THROUGH MY EYES

a story of Hope

To Greg

Bob Whitworth

THROUGH MY EYES

a story of Hope

Bob G. Whitworth

APERIO PRESS
WALNUT CREEK, CALIFORNIA

THROUGH MY EYES
a story of Hope

Bob G. Whitworth
Copyright © 2012 by Bob G. Whitworth
All Rights Reserved

All poetry written by Bob G. Whitworth
All Bible references from the New King James Version unless otherwise noted

Publisher's Cataloging-in-Publication Data
(Provided by Quality Books, Inc.)

Whitworth, Bob G. (Bobby Glenn)
    Through my eyes : a story of hope / Bob G. Whitworth.
-- 1st ed.
    p. cm.
    Includes bibliographical references.
    LCCN 2011961037
    ISBN-13: 978-0-9837875-4-9
    ISBN-10: 0-9837875-4-9

    1. Whitworth, Bob G. (Bobby Glenn) 2. Vietnam War,
1961-1975--Personal narratives, American. 3. Vietnam
War, 1961-1975--Campaigns. 4. Soldiers--Religious life
--United States. I. Title.

DS559.5.W495 2012   959.704'3'092
                           QBI11-600223

10 9 8 7 6 5 4 3 2 1
Printed and bound in the United States of America

Front Cover	Back Cover
Spc4 Bob Whitworth September 25, 1968	Bob Whitworth reflection July 10, 2008
Battle near Tam Ky, Vietnam	Vietnam Memorial Wall, Washington, D.C.
Photo: Dana Stone, AP Worldwide Photos, NY, NY	Photo: Beth Whitworth

I dedicate this book to the soldiers who fought the Vietnam war. They served in the toughest of conditions—extreme heat, rain, mud, darkness, mosquitoes, rats, leeches, snakes, bugs, land mines, snipers, ambushes, friendly fire, and close combat with the enemy. Each of these men walked the daily paths of danger, bearing the stress of injury and death for their brothers-in-arms and country. Even when abandoned by many of their countrymen at home, they stayed the course, showing the strength and courage that few men are forced to find within themselves. I will always consider it a privilege to have served with them.

I also dedicate this to the soldiers in other past wars, who have served our country in its stand for freedom.

Finally, I dedicate this to the soldiers who now stand watch, with fortitude, as we sleep and as we daily go about our busy lives. I salute you for your courage and sacrifice as you face your dangerous task.

Wars are fought on various terrains, and under variable circumstances, but the effect combat has on those who engage in battle remains the same.

TABLE OF CONTENTS

Chapter		Page

INTRODUCTION

I have faced the might of battle and felt the horrors deep,
stunned by its terrors as I gazed on its feats.
Left empty from the impact, drained by the expense;
this is not what I expected before it all began.

At the age of 20, life was wonderful, and a great adventure seemed to be waiting just around the corner.

A tough, tired-looking fellow by the name of John Flat would come by my dad's gas station, where I worked as a kid, and tell us fascinating stories of fighting in the Korean war. He told us of how, while in his foxhole during a battle, he heard a voice say, "Get out of the hole, get out of the hole!" As he quickly crawled to a new position, an artillery shell landed with a deafening explosion where he had just been.

His stories, and movies I'd seen where men fought hard battles and won, made war seem exciting.

One of my high-school buddies had joined the Marines and been killed, which was a little worrisome, but danger always made life more thrilling.

I had not yet learned how deep danger runs.

In reading my stories, I hope you might catch a glimpse of what it was like to be a grunt, a foot soldier during an unpopular war. I trust you will see, through my eyes, the dread, confusion, heartache, despair, relief, humor, and craziness. Understand the adrenalin rush in a soldier's life—always in danger, surviving with fortitude through monsoons, exhaustion, errors, and sleepless nights. It was a time of learning, trusting, and hope as we endured these adversities.

Join me in that adventure, the year that changed my life. It just might change yours, too.

In the world you will have tribulation;
but be of good cheer, I have overcome the world.
John 16:33

Jesus,
horror's thoughts have captured me.
Peace is shallow,
love and mercy have vanished.
Chains have bound my heart.
Fatigue weakens, and doubts whisper.
Confusion stirs my soul.
Evil utters my name,
yet discretion pleads for patience.
Hope prods, and faith moves ahead.

1

SENTRY

Boom! Boom! Boom! Boom! Boom! Boom!

"Stop! Stop!"

Boom! Boom!

"Stop, stop, please, stop!"

In the darkness I watched the flames from my M14 rifle flashing toward the man lying on the ground. He was propped up on one forearm and holding his free hand over his face as he tried to protect himself from the burning powder flashing out of the end of the barrel. I was firing the blank ammunition they had given us to use while playing war games. I stopped shooting because I figured if they had been real bullets, he would have been pretty near dead by now.

"Why did you shoot him?" yelled a big man as he came rushing out of the darkness toward me.

I was an infantry soldier in training out behind Schofield Barracks in the hills of Hawaii. I was on guard duty at the edge of the perimeter we had set up for my infantry company. It was so dark I could hardly see. I had been given orders to stop anyone who came by, check identification, and ask for the evening's password.

"Halt! Who goes there?" I called as someone approached. Breaking protocol, with no hesitation, this guy just kept walking toward me, getting way too close.

"Sergeant of the Guard," he replied.

Wrong answer. Unfortunately for him, the real sergeant of

the guard had just left my position not three minutes earlier. This was not the same guy, so I fired him up. It was fun—the only fun I would ever have shooting a person.

I had just blasted a senior officer of the battalion in charge of our training, and he was not happy about it. He was swearing while the soldiers with him helped him to his feet. He had slipped on the grass and fallen when he tried to quickly back away once I opened up on him. His eyes probably weren't hurt because he was wearing glasses. He was trying to clean the powder off them, and I could see the little black flecks of burnt powder on his face as his assistants turned on their flashlights. I'm sure his face was in a world of hurt.

Wow! Was I going to get out of this or be in a heap of trouble?

I turned to the big guy, who I then could see was our master sergeant, and cautiously told him why I'd shot the intruder. They all just turned and left. The officer must have known he had made a mistake and wanted the encounter to be over. I was just hoping no one had noticed my nametag.

For some reason I had a bad feeling about that senior officer and thought he might be dangerous. Although I didn't know who it was when I opened fire, ultimately I was glad I had this experience.

It was February 1968.

2

HEADED FOR VIETNAM

On April 12, 1968 I was with my platoon aboard an airliner leveling off at 28,000 feet. I was in Second Platoon of Delta Company, 4th Battalion, 21st Infantry, 11th Brigade, Americal Division, United States Army.

There was a crackling noise from the overhead speakers. An authoritative voice announced, "Listen up. You are headed to Vietnam."

Most of us assumed that already. A war had been going on there for years. When I was in high school the Russian Communists had put their missiles in Cuba and President Kennedy had stood up to them. They'd messed with the wrong guy. They had been trying to expand their influence around the world and said they would bury us. Now they were helping the North Vietnamese invade the South, and Kennedy didn't want Communism spreading throughout Vietnam.

He had done something about it and now President Johnson was in charge, continuing the effort. I thought our government was on the right track and trusted that those in power knew what they were doing and would see this war through to the end. I was young and full of energy. I wasn't really afraid of going to war.

I had turned 21 in December of '67. Like most of my friends, I loved fast cars, drag racing, the outdoors, hunting, fishing, movies, and pulling dirty tricks. I liked working on cars, welding, and fabricating all kinds of things. My friends and I made go-carts and scooters together. I also liked making model airplanes and would work for days putting one together. I loved real airplanes too and had been lucky enough to get a ride in a twin-engine Cessna.

Then there were girls. Wow! There were plenty of them at home, but Beth was the one who was special to me as I headed toward Vietnam. She was beautiful, smart, and caring—and that scared me.

My life had been rich and it all happened in the safety of the United States of America.

I'd been drafted after I dropped out of junior college and was sent to Fort Lewis, Washington for basic training. I met Rusty there when I first arrived and we'd hit it off. He was also from California and had played sports growing up. He was in great shape and took to basic training exercise with no problem. Most of the rest of us had some catching up to do to get in shape.

Rusty also had a better handle than I did on knowing when to speak up and when to keep his mouth shut.

"Dress—Right—Dress!" The drill sergeant gave us the command as we were learning about formations in the field. We were supposed to stick our right arm out toward the guy to our right, but I thought it was time for a little humor.

I kicked my heels together, raised my right arm, and yelled, "Heil Hitler!"

The platoon of 35 guys fell apart laughing. I noticed the sergeant quickly turn away with his hand over his mouth, trying to keep from laughing.

His demeanor instantly changed as he turned to face me.

"Whitworth," he yelled as he screwed his face into a deep frown, "you're not going to like what you've got coming your way!"

He was right. I got to scrub the boiler room ceiling for hours that night.

We made it through Basic and, at the end of August, Rusty and I were sent to Fort Polk, Louisiana for Advanced Infantry

Training, better known as AIT. Our plane landed in Shreveport late at night, and when the exit door opened, a wave of heat and humidity hit me like a big elephant fart. Phew! I staggered outside onto the exit ramp, the stagnant night air alive with creature sounds: buzzing, chirping, humming, and the croaking of a frog that sounded big enough to bite my arm off. Instantly, I was covered with sweat, like I'd stepped into a huge sauna. Past the dimly lit runway, the jungle was a wall of darkness that no light penetrated.

That was the first time I'd felt the closeness of night in that manner, with invisible movement stirring around me in its denseness. It didn't take long to wonder if God had set up a big bug-making machine and just left it there, hidden in the swamp, creating hordes of different bugs every day. Which critter was going to get me first? I'd never been away from the West Coast, where the evening air was cool, crisp, and smelled like pine trees, and the night skies were clear and quiet, filled with twinkling stars.

We learned a lot of great stuff in AIT, like how to set up anti-personnel mines, and correctly pull the pin on a hand grenade and throw it without killing ourselves. There was a long list of things they taught us to do, all of which we would have little use for, once we were out of the Army.

First, Second, Third, and Fourth Platoons, each comprised of 30 to 35 soldiers, made up Delta Company. All together there were about 140 of us in Delta Company who, after AIT, went through extended training in the lush green mountains of Hawaii. Those of us in the weapons squad trained on 23-pound .30 caliber M60 machine guns. Since I spent more time with my squad, I got to know them a little better than the rest of the guys in Delta. I liked the camaraderie we had; we were all in this together. We came to know each other for who we were, and the majority of the guys I knew were great.

Every Monday morning we were trucked from Schofield

Barracks out to the hills for training. There we played war games come rain or shine until Friday when we piled our stinky, muddy bodies into trucks for the ride back to the barracks. We were issued passes to go off-base on Saturday and Sunday, so we cleaned the red mud off our gear and spruced up for the weekend.

Plenty of guys spent their free time drinking and partying on Oahu. One of them told me how much fun he was having getting drunk every weekend. This short, wiry guy spoke broken English and always played his music too loud, bobbing and shaking his head to the beat. As far as I was concerned he was out-to-lunch. At 6 a.m. one Sunday morning I walked into the latrine and there he was with his head between two toilets, passed out on the hard tile floor. He'd been pretty sick and had made quite a mess where he lay. His idea of fun didn't look like a good time to me. This was the first time, but it wouldn't be the last, that I would have doubts about this bozo.

The overhead voice continued, "Settle in, it's gonna be a long flight."

We were actually headed to Vietnam, the place we'd heard so much about. Some troops were afraid to go. Just a few days before we left Schofield, one soldier went AWOL and couldn't be found; he had deserted. Two guys in our battalion got drunk and jumped off a barrack's third story walkway and ended up with broken legs. Another tied a rope around his neck and jumped from a building's third story. Evidently the rope broke, as he was found dead the next day in a dumpster directly below where he'd jumped. I wondered if dying in war could be worse than that.

It was a long flight from Hawaii. I knew a few of the guys sitting around me. I looked toward the window seat at Jerry, my machine-gun crew leader. He was from the Chicago area but kinda quiet for a city boy. His mom and girlfriend had flown over to spend a few days before we shipped out. Now his straight, dark hair nearly covered his eyes as his chin rested on his chest. He and a few others were trying to catch a few zzzzs.

Ahead of me sat Fred, aka "Gramps." He was older than the rest of us and had been drafted from Nevada where he worked the family ranch with his widowed mom. It seemed unusual that he got the call under those circumstances. We were an unlikely trio, Jerry, Gramps, and me, but we had spent some time together on a few of those weekend passes. We tried surfing, went to movies and Marine World, found horses to ride, and explored the island.

Frank was someone else in the machine-gun squad who I was just getting to know. He sat across from me with his long legs stretched into the aisle, looking like the lumberjack he was. Drafted from near Seattle, he almost always had a little grin on his face, and his jovial and easy-going nature made it easy for him to make friends.

When our plane landed to refuel in Guam, we weren't allowed to get off although we stood up and milled around a bit. After stretching our legs, we settled back down and the plane took off.

Next stop: Vietnam.

"We'll be landing on a hot LZ," came the announcement over the speakers.

"Hot" meant there would be enemy gunfire coming our way when we arrived at the landing zone.

"Balderdash," I muttered. Our rifles were stuffed in the middle of our duffel bags in the bottom of the plane. I didn't know what to expect when we landed but it certainly didn't make sense that we wouldn't have our weapons if there was going to be enemy fire when we touched down.

Whoever was taking over the speakers couldn't understand what landing in a hot LZ meant… could he?

I was apprehensive but felt calm. I thought I was ready for whatever lay ahead. This was the real deal, the reason we had spent nine months getting ready, the reason we had been trained.

3

IN-COUNTRY

Hours later we approached the runway of the military airfield in Chu Lai, Vietnam, with some of us getting more and more nervous. We could see huge craters that had been blown into the ground outside the barbed wire perimeter. The base was well fortified with heavy bunkers all around.

Whoa! This was it!

When we landed and filed down the steps, my nose was assaulted with an awful stench that filled the air. It was a mixture of jet exhaust and something putrid burning.

What the heck was that?

We lifted our duffel bags off the tarmac and loaded onto the back of the big deuce-and-a-half trucks that had pulled up next to the plane.

As I looked around, it felt strange watching F-4 Phantom jets roaring off with a full bomb load from the same airstrip where we had just landed. However, this was no hot LZ—unless they were talking about the temperature. It wasn't the only time that the intel we were given was different from reality.

Our company stayed in Chu Lai for a week or so to learn more about enemy booby traps and land mines before joining the rest of the battalion at Duc Pho. These mines and booby traps could be found or set off almost anywhere, and it wasn't long before we learned how powerful and dangerous they were. One type of mine the enemy used was called a Bouncing Betty. When you stepped on it, it would bounce up about waist high and explode, killing or terribly maiming you.

Stepping on a mine or setting off a booby trap would become one of the greatest fears we foot soldiers faced. We would soon learn that each step taken could be our last.

We also learned about the enemy we would be fighting: the NVA and the VC, both known to us as "Charlie." The NVA was the North Vietnamese Army. They were spread throughout the mountainous regions of South Vietnam. They were a well-trained army in uniform. The VC or Viet Cong were Vietnamese Communists. They looked and dressed like the local people and would be found mostly in rice paddy country. They were terrorists and worked in small groups, constantly mining the roads and paths. We were informed they would be there to ambush us every chance they got, so we would have to be on the lookout for them all the time.

South Vietnamese soldiers, known as ARVNs, would occasionally assist the American forces in our fight against the NVA or VC. Our platoon ended up not having much contact with them at all.

We were trained that this would be a war fought in the rice paddies, hedgerows, and jungle and would come to realize that we would rarely see the enemy to fight him face-to-face. He would kill and wound us with hidden weapons like pungi pits, booby traps, and land mines he had planted in areas that were totally familiar to him and completely foreign to us.

We learned that he would always be watching us and, just when we thought he couldn't possibly know our location, a sniper's bullet would tell us differently.

When we finished the land-mine and booby-trap training, the company was flown to LZ Bronco,* about 50 miles south of Chu Lai. That was to be our base of operations for the entire

*See map in center of book for this and other locations.

time in-country. We would be loaned out to various outfits to patrol from the coast of the southeast corner of the northern quarter of South Vietnam (designated I Corps) near Duc Pho, north about 100 miles to Da Nang, and west about 70 miles to the mountainous border of Laos.

As we flew southward to our destination, there were mountains far to our right and water as far as we could see on our left. Rice paddies stretched for miles in every direction. We watched as small villages appeared like islands a little higher than the rice paddies. They were scattered throughout the terrain and were surrounded by trees and hedgerows of thick-growing bushes.

LZ Bronco, our "base," "the rear," was located just outside the village of Duc Pho and next to Highway 1, the main road running north and south along the east coast of Vietnam. As we approached, we could see a large green hill surrounded by the base, which covered a huge area. It was beside the highway and we could see the beach of the South China Sea in the near distance.

Rolls of barbed wire filled with trip flares and mines defended the outside edge or perimeter of Bronco. Large, sandbagged bunkers faced out toward the wire, providing cover for men armed with machine guns, rockets, and grenades.

Our helicopters flew around the perimeter and we saw artillery set up at various locations. A Quad-50 sat on the hill in the center of the firebase. This piece of armor had four .50 caliber machine guns set up in front of the gunner's seat, two stacked on the left and two stacked on the right. It was all mounted on a rotating base so the gunner could easily turn toward any location, pull the trigger and fire all four guns, sending four streams of bullets toward the target. The Quad-50 could shoot rounds for thousands of yards and take out armored vehicles with little effort. It would turn a person into hamburger in no time. A gun like this was something to be feared if it was ever turned on you.

LZ Bronco wasn't as large as the Chu Lai Division Headquarters we had just left, but it wasn't a small firebase either. It had an airstrip for supply planes, a staffed hospital, numerous bunkers, groups of tents, helicopters, large storage containers, a mess hall, an outdoor movie screen made of plywood, and storage areas with basic supplies.

Vietnam was hot, humid, and buzzing with mosquitoes all the time. We needed to get acclimated to working in the environment, and the soldiers who were already stationed here in the rear were happy to "help us out" by putting us to work doing anything they didn't want to do themselves.

First we got to fill sandbags and pull KP duty. Then they were especially happy to have us do everyone's least favorite job: take the barrels from the outdoor latrines, add diesel fuel, light them on fire, and stir the contents until the waste had burned. What a smell those "honey buckets" gave the camp! Fort Polk in Louisiana smelled sweet compared to this. But they could pose a great danger—if the barrels were left burning or smoking in the evening, they provided the enemy with a sighting point where mortars could be aimed. The Viet Cong frequently fired from the tree line and were always probing the perimeter at night to find a weakness, trying to get through our defenses and onto the base.

The foot soldiers, aka "grunts," who had been in-country about six months, were considered old guys and loved to tell us about their worst experiences just to watch us squirm. Most of them were no more than 19 or 20. Their war stories were always horrific—like someone getting his head blown off or getting lost from his unit on patrol, only to be found cut to pieces the next day. Unfortunately, these weren't exaggerations.

I watched a bunch of them move out one evening to set up

a small ambush and I was there the next morning when they returned. Several of them were bandaged up. It was obvious things had gone wrong. It left me thinking that these horrific deeds happened every single day.

I had some learning to do.

4

FIRST DAY IN THE FIELD

Fear is a strange thing and often comes with the unknown. It can come out of nowhere and set in on you like hot, sticky tar. No matter what you do, it won't leave.

That happened to me as soon as we stepped outside the perimeter fence of LZ Bronco on our first in-country patrol looking for any sign of the enemy. I couldn't shake the fear and decided I would just have to wait it out—there was no other choice. I wondered if I was the only one who felt it so strongly.

We had been at Bronco for about a week when our company was ordered to head out. We packed full rucksacks and formed a line to head through the perimeter fence eastward toward the sea. We had all been issued our basic gear. Our rucksacks held everything considered necessary to survive.

We each had a poncho that we could wear in the rain. If we found a couple of long sticks, we could snap two ponchos together and make a small shelter. We had a poncho liner, which was a lightweight blanket that dried quickly, and a rugged one-man air mattress. When it rained at night, it could keep us out of the water and mud and help make the ground more even. Personal stuff, like a toothbrush, shaver, comb, towel, and soap, was also included. Our meals consisted mainly of C-rations (awful canned food), and we sometimes needed to carry three days' worth. The Army made an effort to send us a hot meal whenever they could get a chopper to us, but those meals were sporadic.

We packed a trip flare and a Claymore anti-personnel mine

with a detonator, which were staples to use on ambushes or to help protect our perimeter. We carried a small folding shovel called a trenching tool. This either went into the rucksack or hooked to our pistol belt along with two single-quart canteens of water and a pouch containing a bandage.

A soldier in each platoon was designated as the radio-telephone operator (RTO) and would carry our communications radio, which weighed 25 pounds, besides his own gear. Two soldiers each carried a 23-pound M60 machine gun and 200 rounds of 7.62mm ammo. An M16 was standard issue with 180 rounds of 5.56mm ammo. Because I was in the machine-gun squad, when it was my turn to carry the M60, I added a .45 caliber pistol in a holster to my belt for backup. Most of us carried extra ammo as well as two to four hand grenades. I really liked grenades; they weren't precision weapons—you only had to get 'em close.

We carried gas masks and wore a heavy flack-vest that would stop small shrapnel, but not a bullet. Because of the heat and extra weight, it didn't take long for most of us to get rid of our vests. Last, we each wore a metal helmet. In total, we carried 70 to 80 pounds or more. When we went on short patrols or ambushes, we didn't take our rucksacks, but most of the time we carried them. We lived out of those packs.

I had grown up in farm country and worked in the fields some, but had never seen a rice paddy until I arrived in Vietnam. At this time of year they were just fields covered with water. Here I was on our first patrol, walking on a narrow dirt dike that separated the paddies. It had been drilled into us that the enemy would booby-trap these dikes.

Why were we walking on them?

It didn't make a whole lot of sense. Besides that, we were in the open and I kept thinking we were great targets if bullets started flying our way, since we didn't have any cover. All we would be able to do was splat down in the muddy water. But maybe someone leading us across these wide-open fields knew something I didn't.

We stayed strung out in one long line until we broke into our individual platoons to patrol villages as well as the paddies. Everything went fine. We encountered no snipers or booby traps. It took us until evening to reach the beach.

The endless stretch of white sand and beautiful blue water came as a surprise. It reminded me of the Southern California coastline. The air smelled salty and gulls squalled and dipped in a bit of a breeze coming off the water. It looked like a tropical vacation destination—all it needed were thatched huts and bathing beauties.

We were given our nighttime positions where we dug foxholes in the sand. We sat with our backs to the water. Out in front of us about 300 yards was a tree line and brush. We were to watch the tree line for the enemy that night. Since we were all new to this and pretty nervous, we didn't know what to expect. We kept seeing little lights blinking in the dark and weren't sure what they were.

What if they were the enemy smoking cigarettes?

Wanting to be safe rather than sorry, we fired at the little lights until dawn. It rained on us off and on throughout the night and filled our foxholes with water. In the morning, I was soaking wet and had sand in every crevice of my body. Man, oh man, was I miserable!

It turned out that the little lights we had seen were just fireflies. We had fired so much ammo that word came down we couldn't shoot the next night without permission. In one of our platoons just down the beach however, things had gone very poorly that first night.

Their platoon had set up a forward position in front of their perimeter. A soldier was sent out to man that position and tied a string to his hand to keep him in touch with the guard position behind him. Sometime during the night he fell asleep and the string came off his hand. Contact was lost. Later he stood up without identifying himself and nervous soldiers at the guard position took him for the enemy and fired, killing him.

Surely this was a bad start.

5

ALL-NIGHT AMBUSH

Being on an ambush in the middle of the night can be very frightening. When you're new at it, there is a lot to worry about.

Did the VC see you go into your position? Will everyone be quiet? Will they stay awake? What about snakes? What if too many VC come down the trail?

Orders had come down from battalion headquarters that ambushes had to be set up nightly while we were in the field. At dusk, every platoon sent out a squad to set up an all-night ambush. Six to eight soldiers heavily armed with machine guns, grenades, rockets, and Claymore mines went to a predetermined location after dark to hide along a path and wait. If the enemy came along, we set off the ambush.

We were looking for the Viet Cong who worked the more populated areas and villages where we were operating. They ran in small groups and seemed to act sporadically. They would often wait until dark, come out of hiding, and go into the small villages. We didn't know exactly why; perhaps they were visiting their wives. We knew that they would also use the cover of darkness as a time to force the villagers to replenish their supplies.

The first time I was chosen to go on an ambush, I went with six other soldiers from Second Platoon. We picked a site 25 feet away from a trail that led out of one of the villages. For our cover, we had short piles of cut sugarcane in front of us, and seven-foot high cane stalks growing behind us, which made it difficult for us to be seen. Frank, the lumberjack from Seattle, was on my left. Four or five other guys were strung out to my right.

I couldn't see very far because it was dark. There were always plenty of mosquitoes buzzing around, looking for their chance to feed on us and leave itchy bumps all over if we weren't smeared with insect repellent. We had been lying and watching most of the night and my eyes burned from making myself stay awake. Ambushes often were long, scary hours of waiting with nothing to do but watch, listen, and think about how we had ended up here. It was easy to be restless, but dangerous if we were noisy.

Around 0400 hours we heard noises.

"There they are," someone to my right whispered.

Even though I couldn't see much, I pulled the pins and threw my hand grenades. After the blast of my last grenade I raised up to fire my M16.

KABOOM!

A horrendous explosion went off right in front of me, forcing my head back. Shrapnel ripped into the small cane pile I was behind and pieces of metal screamed past my head, cutting both sides of my face as it crashed into the tall cane behind me.

Dang!

I wasn't sure where that had come from. The sides of my face were burning from the cuts and I could feel blood on my cheeks.

Wow! That was too close!

I lay back down behind the pile of cane. My body must have kicked in so much adrenalin that I felt no fear.

"Hey, Frank!" I called out. "Throw those grenades a little farther!"

I doubted Frank had thrown his grenade short, but it was worth mentioning.

"Oh, sure Bob," Frank replied. "Sorry about that."

In my mind's eye I could see that little grin on his face.

To this day, he and I still chuckle about my initiation to the effects of a juggernaut.

At the time though, I groggily sat up and fired my M16 blindly into the darkness out in front of our position along with everyone else. Then it was quiet. This whole thing happened in mere seconds. I jammed a full clip into my M16, listened, and waited. It was very important to be still and quiet. Our position had been briefly exposed and we needed to stay there until dawn.

At first light we carefully looked over the surrounding area. We couldn't find any bodies. We moved out and headed back to our platoon. When we got there, a medic looked at my cuts and cleaned them up. Word got around that I had some small wounds.

Gramps, my other good buddy, had to get in his two cents' worth of Nevada cowboy complaints.

"What are yuh trying to do, Whitworth, get yer head blowed off? You fruitcake! Don't yuh know you're supposed to duck after you throw those gol-durn things?"

"Wipe that big smile off your face, Gramps," I replied.

"You just wanna be the first guy in the company to get a Purple Heart," he muttered as he walked off.

At the time I hardly knew what a Purple Heart was; I was just very thankful that the shrapnel hadn't done worse damage. All the platoons joined together again and we headed back to LZ Bronco.

6

THIS AIN'T NO MOVIE

As soon as we got to LZ Bronco, I developed a high fever and was admitted to the hospital. Outside the entrance was a large asphalt pad where huey helicopters landed and took off. I passed a sandbagged bunker just before I walked through the door. The ward was long and narrow, with beds lined on each side beginning at the door, and a walkway down the middle. Behind the beds on the left was an identical ward, separated by a wooden wall three or four feet tall. From the top of this short wall to the ceiling was a bug screen made of metal. In that ward were sick or hurt Vietnamese.

My bed was the fourth from the door. In the bed next to mine was a guy I knew as Romeo. He had been our captain's driver when we trained in Hawaii. Romeo had an IV in his left arm that was running into his vein too quickly. This had caused his arm to swell twice the size it should have been and it looked painful. We both felt lousy so there wasn't much conversation.

By the second or third day my fever wasn't going away and the medics still had no idea what was causing it. After resting all day, Romeo and I fell asleep. I have no idea what time it was, but sometime in the middle of the night we were awakened by loud explosions getting closer and louder. The lights had gone out and it was pitch black. Jarred awake by the blasts, we rolled out of our beds and onto the floor.

One of the first things a combat soldier learns is that when you realize hostile fire is coming your way, the safest place to be is as close to the ground as possible. Once there, you can decide what to do next. This becomes second nature and it can take 20 or 30 years to get over it, if ever. We quickly realized that mortars were being "walked" into the hospital, each one getting closer by the second.

Romeo was having trouble moving his IV pole. As I jumped up off the floor, he grabbed the pole and began to run with me down the walkway with the IV jar swinging on its hook. As we ran, the mortars were coming through the tin roof behind us, exploding and blowing the roof and bug screens apart. Shrapnel was flying everywhere with pieces whizzing past us and hitting almost everything. It was unbelievable! It was like what I had seen in the movies. But this wasn't a movie, or even a bad dream. It was real!

Here we were, trying to outrun the incoming mortars, moving as fast as we could in our hospital pajamas, having no idea what else to do but run, IV and all. I heard gunfire outside on the perimeter.

What if Charlie makes it through the barbed wire? What if they make it past the bunker line inside our defenses?

This was no time to be without a weapon. It was truly one of those times when I wondered if I was in over my head. I didn't know what to do. It was easy to visualize myself splattered across the ward in pieces of bloody pale blue hospital pajamas. I never dreamed I might die like that. We just needed a hole we could drop into so we wouldn't be blown to kingdom come.

As we ran through the hospital in the dark, we came to an intersection between the wards and plowed full speed into a big three-foot diameter fan. It had been set up on a pole in the center of the intersection to blow down the walkway. The fan crashed onto the floor and we tumbled over it. The mortars, which had continued falling past us, suddenly stopped.

Somehow Romeo got back up without losing his IV. I got up too. The explosions started again and were heading back in our direction! We couldn't quit now! We hardly knew what to do, so we turned around and ran for our lives. We dashed back through the ward and outside into the sand-bagged bunker. The last mortars fell too close for comfort as we dove through the door. Now we waited with a few others in the safety of our shelter. We could hear gunfire, slowly dying down, coming from the outside bunker line near the perimeter. Soon it was all over. Romeo and I had made it through without a scratch.

I wondered what damage had been done and who had been hurt, so I left the bunker and turned down a passageway between two buildings. Even though it was dark I could see a soldier about my age sprawled out on the dirt walkway. He had been hit during the attack and although there were no gaping wounds or blood, he was dead. Another soldier showed up and went for a stretcher.

While he was gone I realized that this could have been me. I just stood there staring. When the soldier returned with the stretcher, we lifted the body onto it and carried it inside, leaving the dead soldier in the ward. This was the first time I had ever picked up a dead person. It surprised me. There was no feeling of life in him. No matter how we handled him, he never moved, not even a breath. It was so final.

I headed back to my bed. When I got there, dim lights were on and I could see the bug screen across from my bed had been blown full of holes and was shredded. Parts of the metal roof had been blown off and blood was spattered all around. I could hear crying and moaning coming from up and down the Vietnamese ward.

The reality of war was sinking in. I felt numb.

In the morning I wanted to leave. I still wasn't doing that well, but they said they'd let me go anyway. The hospital, with Hueys parked so close, seemed like too big a target to me. I wanted to be back with my buddies. Heck, what had happened on my first ambush seemed like nothing compared to last night, and I didn't want to be in this type of place without a weapon.

I had grown up around guns. I went on my first hunt when I was about three. My grandma lived outside of town and often watched my two older brothers and me. When our uncles came around they liked to go rabbit hunting, so to give Grandma a break, they would take us with them. We would leave the house and walk out into the desert. I remember reaching up to hold my Uncle Bill's finger as we walked along. When the rabbits jumped out of the bushes, my uncles would shoot at the running targets. That was big stuff for a little guy like me. As I'd grown older, I hunted rabbits a lot, mainly because there wasn't much else to do in our little town.

This was no rabbit hunt. I was learning fast, and knew I had no guarantee I would make it through the next 11 months. I left the hospital and soon found my platoon along the bunker line next to the base perimeter.

"How'd it go last night?" I asked Jerry, my Chicago-raised machine-gun crew leader.

"There was shooting along the bunker line during the mortar attack, but no real problems," he replied.

I didn't say anything about what I had been through because I didn't know how to explain what I'd seen or how it felt.

It was the first of several mortar attacks I experienced. There was no fighting back. No tough-guy stuff. It was a very helpless feeling to realize the only thing you could do is not be there. Running or hiding helped, and the quicker you got moving the better. If you were caught too close to the falling mortars, you wouldn't have time to realize that you were no more.

The night before was another eye-opener. Death literally dropped out of the sky with no warning, turning what I had thought would be a safe night's sleep into a waking nightmare. I had a churning feeling in my belly that the days ahead may turn into something I never expected.

Wearing hospital pajamas still gives me the urge to run and hide.

7

LOST

When you walked through elephant grass, you were constantly surrounded by the loud, high-pitched noise of thousands of cicada bugs. The sound was everywhere, and unsettling as it went on all day. When we were on patrol, everybody in the platoon had to take his turn walking "point." The assignment was made in the morning before we started.

The point man walked at the head of the patrol with the next man following about 20 to 40 yards behind him. From there, each man kept a distance of three to five yards between them. Sometimes there would be a flank man on the point man's right or left, if conditions allowed. The point man periodically made eye contact with the man behind him, so if he spotted trouble he could signal back to let the platoon know. If he tripped a booby trap, the others would be far enough behind to miss the blast. If he walked into the enemy while in brush or high grass, they might think he was the only one, and the shooting would start with just him, warning the others behind to take cover.

No matter where we were, the point man had to keep his eyes peeled for everything. It was a dangerous and nerve-wracking job that was nearly impossible when we were in elephant grass that was nine to ten feet high. The man on point had to decide whether to chop his way through with a machete or walk on a path made by someone else. It was slow going and exhausting to chop through the grass in the heat, but using someone else's path often proved very dangerous.

When we were sent out into the field like this, our day

typically started by getting up at dawn to a C-ration breakfast. *Yummy!*

There was a sure-fire way to have myself a hot breakfast. I always carried an extra Claymore mine. I would break it apart, take out the pound of C-4 plastique and dump the case. A marble-sized little ball of the explosive burned hot and could easily be lit—even in the rain. This worked great for heating up C-ration cans. The remaining plastique went into one of the outside pockets on my rucksack for later use.

Most mornings I had instant coffee, canned eggs with chopped ham, and some B-3 cookies with a chocolate or vanilla center. Those cookies lasted forever. They didn't deteriorate or melt in the sun. It wasn't long before my sweet tooth and I were ready to trade or argue to get those awful cookies.

After breakfast was over, we were ordered to get ready to move out. Jerry informed me that it was my turn to walk point. Frank, with a wad of chewing tobacco in his lower lip, was sitting next to a bush nearby, looking at me with that silly little grin on his face.

"Hmm, are you sure? I think its Frank's turn," I said, stalling a little and hoping to make Frank whine.

At 0700 hours I started through the elephant grass at the head of the platoon. The area was flat with a lot of trails running through it. To my left there were hills slowly rising up. The tall grass became thinner in that direction. Lt. John, who was assigned to Second Platoon when we arrived in Vietnam, had sent Joe, someone I barely knew, to walk on my left flank maybe 25 yards away. Walking down a trail through the tall, dense grass, I was able to keep Joe in and out of my sight. The bozo from the latrine was back about 30 yards behind me. He was my connection to the platoon so I frequently looked back at him.

The lieutenant usually called for a break about two hours into our patrol, and even though we'd been hard at it for at least that long, Bozo hadn't signaled any word from the platoon. It was getting hotter by the hour. He was the only person I could see behind me, which was what I expected. Every now and then I caught a glimpse of Joe. I knew he was depending on me to stay in touch with the rest of the platoon—and with good reason.

Two days earlier one of the guys in our battalion had become separated from his platoon while on patrol and got lost. His body was found on a bridge the next morning—covered with cigarette burns and a note stuck to him saying "G.I. GO HOME."

I kept following the trail farther into the tall grass, being as careful as I could. I just hoped Bozo was paying attention behind me because I had to stay alert to the trail. I listened for sounds and looked for anything out of place: trip wires, freshly moved earth, movement, or some sign that would give me a hint of danger—anything that appeared out of the ordinary.

After another hour I stopped and motioned for Joe to come over. When Bozo caught up with us, and no one else was following him, I couldn't believe it.

"Where is the rest of the platoon?" I asked.

He just looked at me.

"Oh, man, they stop a long time ago. I tol' 'em I wanna go wi' chew."

His words slammed into me like a charging water buffalo.

I looked over at Joe and could see the anger in his eyes. He knew just what that meant. We were lost. We didn't have a map or a radio, and I have always had a bad sense of direction. We could only guess how long ago the platoon had stopped. Being in the elephant grass was like being in a massive maze. The trails broke off in all directions.

I knew what Joe was thinking because I was thinking it too. This guy was an idiot. Why not shoot this bozo right here and now or just beat the living daylights out of him? But, if we did that, we could give away our location to "unfriendlies." Bozo didn't even know we were lost, and dealing with him would just create more problems. Forget him.

With Joe right behind me, I took off back down the trail, only guessing which way to turn. The grass was so tall I couldn't see up and over it. Frequently we would come to a fork in the trail, and I would have to make a wild guess which way to go. We would hurry a ways down that path and come to another fork. By 1100 hours, I was sure we were lost.

Being lost pretty much terrified me. I had decided I would never be captured, no matter what. I was of the opinion that a low-level grunt like me becoming a prisoner would only result in a slow, torturous death at the enemy's hand. I wasn't ready now, and maybe never would be, to have my commitment tested, which drove me to quickly find our platoon. This only increased the danger because I gave no caution to booby traps or other hazards in my intensified pace. I knew that if we were still lost come dark, things would get much worse. Joe stayed right on my heels and Bozo dragged along behind us.

Finally, five panic-filled hours later, we broke into a clearing and spotted our men. We hadn't stopped at all the entire time. Our shirts were soaked with sweat, and we were exhausted from the pace we had kept in the blistering heat.

The lieutenant was relieved to see us but was instantly furious. He headed straight at me yelling about my heritage, saying I didn't have a legitimate father and my mother had been a bad woman. He also told me I was the part of the body where poop came out, as well as many other things. I held back from telling him that I liked him too. I suspected he wouldn't have understood. I was just elated to be back with the platoon, even if it meant I had to listen to him chewing on me.

I actually thought Bozo should have gotten the reaming and I should have received a medal for finding our way back, but for some reason he didn't give a hoot about Bozo. Lt. John wasn't the only one who was upset. All the rest of the guys were mad too because they had been searching for us the whole scorching day. I walked over to the gun crew and Frank looked at me with that little grin on his face. It was a great thing to see, but he was the only one smiling.

Years later, when my son was learning to talk and I'd be leaving the house, he would look up at me and say, "Daddy, I wanna go with you!" That innocent voice would trigger the memory of Bozo's words, and they would echo through my mind.

8

LESSONS LEARNED

We had been patrolling all day. We stopped for a break in the shade of some tall coconut trees, trying to get some relief from the hot sun. Guys lit up smokes or dug some old snack out of their packs, washing it down with warm water from their canteens. The days of getting cold drinks from a refrigerator seemed gone forever.

Bruce somehow ended up with a coconut off one of the trees, busted it open, and was doing his best to get the meat out of it. He had been drafted from somewhere along the Columbia River on the Washington/Oregon border. He was one of the guys I counted on to have my back. He was always generous, offering to lend a hand when it was time to carry the heavy stuff.

Lt. John walked past me with four guys.

"Whitworth, come with us!" he ordered.

I followed, and we eventually ended up walking along a wide path at the bottom of the hill. The lieutenant turned to me.

"Whitworth, I want you to remember this place because you are going to lead some guys back here for an ambush tonight."

That seemed strange because I had never been asked to lead anything or anybody anywhere the whole time I had been in the Army, except on the days when I walked point.

Maybe he had changed his mind about me even though he had talked dirty to me for a half-hour for being lost just a few days earlier. I had managed to find our way back, which was pretty good for me, seeing as how I had such a poor sense of direction. He probably didn't really mean all those foul names he had called me.

Lt. John pointed to the exact location of our up-coming ambush. I didn't care for the site he had chosen, but he wasn't asking, he was telling. After all, he was the "boss." Officers looked at things differently than we did, but they had orders to follow just the same. As far as I knew, the Army infantry chain of command started with the lieutenant colonel in charge of the battalion. He gave orders to the captain who was in charge of our company, which consisted roughly of 140 soldiers broken into four platoons. The captain passed orders down through the four platoon lieutenants. We called some of them "90-Day Wonders" because most of them had gotten only 90 days' training at Officer Candidate School before becoming an officer. Often times, new infantry lieutenants lasted only about three weeks in the field before they were killed because of their inexperience.

The lieutenant gave orders to the platoon sergeant, usually ranked E6 or E7, who passed those orders down to the four squad leaders, usually buck sergeants ranked E5. The squad leader then passed the orders to his seven-man squad comprised of specialist E4s and privates.

That was me, Private Bob. I was at the bottom of the chain of command. I don't think it gets any lower unless you're in jail.

While we were in Hawaii, our captain had introduced us to the concept that the officers weren't running a popularity contest when giving orders. However, we lowly grunts knew we needed to read between the lines to figure out how to get the job done and not end up dead. I didn't have much experience in fighting a war, but I had learned a few things in my earlier years about finding help when none seemed available.

When I was a kid, I'd been small for my age. There had always seemed to be someone bigger or tougher than me who wanted to cause trouble. That had gotten me into several fights when I was growing up, and things always seemed to turn out differently than I had planned.

Once, a kid named Raymond and his friends had been picking on a buddy of mine. Kenny was having a tough time of it. His dad was a cool guy but had been killed in a terrible truck accident two years before. It had been my first encounter with death, and was really tough on me, so there was no telling what it was doing to Kenny. The passage of time had helped a little, but his dad's death had surely put a dent in his self-confidence. I stepped in to help with this fight, and much to my surprise, my friend had stepped back and left the fight to me.

Right off the bat, Raymond and I had come to blows, and I didn't make much headway. We were at school and the bell rang, so the fight stopped. I didn't think it was over though, because Raymond's pals were giving him a hard time about not having been able to kick my butt. I'd gotten away that day without further trouble, but I hadn't planned on being in this by myself.

This isn't over yet.

I was about 11 at the time and realized I needed some advice. So I rode my bike over to my dad's gas station.

After he listened to my story there was a short silence.

"Bobby," he told me, "I don't know what you should do. You need to figure it out."

I silently screamed, *"No, Dad!"*

I had been hoping for more of an answer, but that was it. I was on my own. I was extremely disappointed and left the gas station right away.

I knew that Dad prayed for answers he didn't have, so I decided to give it a try. I had done this before and it hadn't seemed to work very well, but being *really* serious this time, I made a request.

"Jesus, I need some help. I don't know what to do, and I don't want to get my rear kicked at school. Would you please help me? Amen."

I assumed He knew all about my troubles.

The next day at school, things seemed pretty normal. But when I went to get my bike after school, Raymond and his buddies were there, waiting for me.

Well, it's time to face the music.

I discovered, to my surprise, that Raymond had no interest in tangling with me. His buddies were giving him a hard time, but he didn't care. He just wanted it to be over. As I got on my bike, I wondered if my prayer had helped.

I was slowly learning what my dad knew. He had surely sized up the problem correctly by staying out of it, and unknowingly sent me to the same place he went to for help.

In this war-torn country, as I thought about leading the guys to the ambush that night, I began to get the feeling I was going to need some of that same kind of help sooner rather than later.

After the lieutenant showed us the ambush location, he led us back to the rest of the platoon and we all headed up the hill. When we arrived at the top, we saw a wide flat place that had been cleared. It looked big enough for a chopper to land. We dropped our rucksacks and took a long break before we started setting up the nighttime perimeter.

When it was dusk, Lt. John walked up to me.

"Whitworth," he said, "be ready to move out."

It was getting dark quickly, and we were ready to go, but there were 16 of us, twice as many as we needed. I went to the sergeant who had been put in charge.

"Why are so many of us going down there?" I asked.

He ignored me.

By the time we left, it was completely dark. Word was that "everybody" had mined the hill we were about to stumble down: the Japanese, the French, the Viet Cong, and the U.S.A. Well, that was almost everybody.

It was so dark it was almost impossible to see. The first guy behind me slid his hand into my pistol belt and followed me down the hill. One after another, all 14 behind him did the same. There were lots of bushes to trip over, and the trees seemed to make it even darker. There was plenty to worry about, and fear settled in my gut.

Earlier, in the daylight, I had seen several old punji-pits whose camouflaged covers had been worn away by weather. The pits were triangular-shaped holes about three feet on each side and 18-feet deep, with two-foot-long sharp wooden stakes sticking up from the bottom. The wooden stakes were often smeared with human dung to cause infection in the wounds of whoever fell on them. In addition, the VC had learned how to put explosives at the bottom of the pits. That could give an unfortunate soldier quite a lift.

I had seen many of these pits in the area where we were headed, but the real problem I worried about was the ones I hadn't seen and couldn't see now.

We kept stumbling down the hill without setting off a mine. Somehow, we finally reached the wide path I had been shown earlier. I could barely make out where some of the old punji-pits were. What I would have given for a flashlight, but that might have meant death by giving away our position.

Once we reached the path, I turned left and we moved slowly along like a big snake. In the darkness, we tried our best not to fall over each other or into a pit. After a short time, I could tell we had arrived at the spot the lieutenant had shown me earlier in the day. We made another turn and walked up a three-foot-high dirt rise, and through a small opening in the short brush growing there. Behind the brush, the ground was flat, going back toward the hill we had just come down.

We stood in a 30-foot square clearing, with taller bushes and trees growing on the other three sides of its perimeter. The hill in front of us was dense, with very tall trees and brush casting dark shadows over the path, making it virtually impossible to see if someone was there.

Planning to ambush the Viet Cong as they came along the path, the sarge ended up putting all 16 of us in the flat area.

Since I was only a private, he wasn't interested in my ideas, even though I was the only one who had seen the site in daylight. The three-man machine-gun crew was set up in a corner with the gun facing the only small opening in the brush where we had entered. I was in the left corner opposite the gun crew with my Claymores facing out toward the path where we expected the VC to travel. Five guys were staring back at the hill of trees we had come down, with their backs to the path. The other six guys, including the sarge, were huddled in a couple different groups, with nowhere specifically to shoot. The area was just too small to accommodate that many people effectively. This was chaos waiting to happen in the dark.

I lay down, holding one Claymore detonator in each hand. If I set off these mines, anyone on the path would be killed. The medic was right next to me.

"If anything happens, don't go backwards," I told him. "Right behind us are three old punji-pits."

Meanwhile, the sarge had sent Rex, a smart fella from Pennsylvania with a California attitude, along with three others out through the small opening to set up trip-flares. They were supposed to tie the flare to a limb, or whatever they could find, run a wire from it across to the other side of the path, and tie it off. They had to do this in the dark and had been out there far too long.

Were they still out there?

Someone tripped a flare and the path lit up. The small bushes were in the way so I couldn't see clearly who it was. I heard yelling and movement in front of me on the path. I snapped the safeties off the Claymore detonators in my hands and started to squeeze.

Should I? Shouldn't I? Should I? Shouldn't I? No! That's not the VC! They couldn't have gotten here yet, could they?

I glanced to my right, where figures came running through the small opening back toward us. The machine gunner opened up on them, thinking they were VC. I saw tracer bullets flashing between the screaming shadows as they came toward the clearing. Somehow they got past the machine-gun fire without being hit, and the shooting stopped. It was Rex and the others we had almost killed. I could hear someone hollering behind me.

"Help! Help me!"

I edged back, and knew the screams were coming from one of the old punji-pits. I moved closer and looked into the dark hole. The medic had moved backward in the commotion and fallen into the pit. He was dangling from the edge, barely hanging on to the side. I quickly grabbed his arm and hand and pulled him up and onto the ground next to me.

I left him there in the dark panting madly, trying to catch his breath, and crawled back over to my position. I found the mine detonators and flattened myself on the ground.

As I lay there in the darkness, my heart was trying to beat its way out of my chest. It was hard to be still. I had been a split second from blowing Rex and the other guys away; then we almost shot them. I realized the VC didn't have to kill us; we could do a pretty good job of that ourselves.

The stupidity of what had just happened was borderline insanity, and the severity of the situation filled me with fear and frustration.

There was so much incompetence. How could I get past it? I didn't want to accept that I might really die, but I knew it was possible, especially in the confusion of events like what had just happened. I didn't know how to accept what was going on.

I was a soldier, but still thinking the way a civilian would.

Did I need to give up all my plans for going home despite my hope that I could survive?

The Book of Proverbs in the Bible says to be not afraid of sudden terror.[1] I had to take confidence in that. It was starting to sink in; I was getting a taste of how tough it was going to be to live through this year.

At home, there had been little troubles like being broke,

getting in a fistfight with someone a little bigger than me, or maybe getting a speeding ticket. But here in Vietnam, things were seriously crazy.

The main word was "kill!" We were here to kill the enemy, as was drilled into us in basic training.

"What's the spirit of the bayonet, soldier?" the drill sergeant yelled.

"To kill, Sarge! To kill!" we yelled back.

Not only was death the main objective, we were forced to rely on the wisdom and ingenuity of those who were ranked higher than we were to make good decisions about our safety. This didn't come easily to me. I didn't trust a guy just because he was a lieutenant. I learned early not to assume that because someone was in leadership they would do the right thing.

As a little guy, I had learned a couple of lessons that stuck with me. The first one took place when I was about four.

Word had spread through the neighborhood that kids were meeting at the school down the street to play baseball. When the time came, Johnny, who I'd known since we'd learned how to walk, and I decided we'd like to play. We joined a group of boys around our age and a little older, who also wanted to play. The local P.E. coach was there to make this happen. He picked two boys to be captains and told them to each take turns picking teammates. The captains kept picking kids and the group to choose from had gotten smaller and smaller. Soon there had been only Johnny and me left.

"Okay, let's go play ball!" the coach said.

The two of us had watched as he led the chosen teams toward the field. It was obvious we hadn't been picked. What had just happened?

The coach hadn't said anything like, "Sorry, guys, but we have enough players for two teams now," or, "You two need a little more time to grow; when you're bigger I'll try to get you on a team." Nothing was said. We were simply left standing there.

Even at that young age, I had known something was wrong.

I didn't understand how everything worked, but I knew about sportsmanship and fairness, and they had not been a part of what had just happened.

That experience was one of the main reasons I almost never played sports as a kid, which was my loss, because kids learn many good principles when playing sports. You learn how to set goals, make plans, do what's best for the team and yourself, be disciplined, have sportsmanship, and work together to smooth out the bumps. But I'd learned what I might expect from people—a lesson that would pay high dividends in the future.

The second lesson that stuck with me came about when I was almost five and had just started kindergarten. Things had been going well and I liked school. I'd been in my class for a few hours, and it was time to color. We formed a small line, and Randy, the boy in front of me, picked a box of crayons. Almost instantly he'd been unhappy with them and wanted a different box.

Our teacher, standing right next to us, smiled at him.

"No, Randy, keep those."

Randy went into a rage and threw the crayons on the floor.

I thought Randy might have something coming after that, but didn't expect it would happen so fast. Instantly, the teacher grabbed Randy with one hand, lifted him off the floor, and began beating the fire right out of his rear.

I'd known I was way too close to the action and, thinking I might get hit by accident, started backing away as fast as I could. The teacher dropped Randy on the floor, and after a while he'd stopped crying, gathered his box of crayons, and stood there like a good boy.

I got the message loud and clear. My kindergarten teacher had demonstrated how quickly situations could be changed by those in power. I learned that when things weren't going well, or if something didn't look right, I'd better be alert.

My experience with the P.E. teacher had taught me that just

because I thought something should happen a certain way didn't mean it would, right or wrong. Both lessons had shown me that because someone was older, bigger, or in charge, did not mean they could be trusted to do what I thought was correct.

I was under the influence of powerful people in the military, some wise, some foolish; and the enemy was always around, looking for ways to take advantage of our mistakes. The lessons I had learned as a very little boy applied now more than ever.

So, lying there in our ambush site, having given our position away and almost killing some of our own guys, I felt like we were sitting ducks. The sarge sat a little bit away from me. I heard him talking quietly over the radio.

"We've compromised our ambush site. Request permission to move."

"Negative," the voice on the radio replied, "hold your position."

Sarge handed the mike back to the RTO.

"We're holding this position," he told us.

I could hear information coming over the radio.

"Concentrated VC attacks in your area."

I saw flares fired from the direction of our base. They left trails of light and exploded high up in the air, causing the night sky and the ground to look as though it was daytime. I was already more scared than I had been in my life. I knew fear could take little problems and turn them into big ones, but these were already big problems.

Now what?

I was doing my best to stay under control. I wondered if the voice coming over the radio had been talking to us.

How did he know where we were? Surely he wasn't warning us, was he?

I tried to settle in for the long night ahead, praying for us to myself, and trying to trust we'd be okay.

I lay there with the two detonators in my hands, staring out into the darkness. There were always strange noises at night: snapping, crushing, and stepping sounds. Maybe it was just animals moving around, but it was enough to keep a new guy like me worried all night. Even so, we made it until morning without further incident.

9

FOOLS RUSH IN

In the morning, we headed back along the path and up the hill to the rest of the platoon. David, from Third Squad, and I were talking about the night before and decided to ask Lt. John about improving the way these ambushes were pulled off. David accompanied us on more than his share of ambushes, as he was the only one trained on a starlight scope.

We started walking across the clearing at the top of the hill, and I noticed Bozo tying a thin rope to a piece of wet cardboard sticking up out of the ground. After getting lost with him, needless to say, I wanted nothing to do with him. Curious about what he was up to, David and I stood and watched from a safe distance as he stepped back about 50 feet, lay on the ground, and pulled the rope. As he pulled on the rope, a little piece of cardboard tore off. Swearing, he walked back over and tied it again. He repeated this several times. Each time he pulled the rope he crouched a little higher up off the ground. Soon he was just standing.

We got bored watching him, so we headed over behind a large boulder to talk with Lt. John about the ambush. The lieutenant didn't seem too happy to see me. I had barely started to mention some of our ideas when he suddenly jumped in the air, grabbed his helmet, and slammed it to the ground.

"Whitworth, you S-O-B!" he hollered.

He continued with his yelling: about my dad being no good, my mother spending time with men other than my dad, and me having my head up my butt. It was the same kind of stuff he had said to me before, but this time his speech included something about an air strike he had witnessed, and what had happened there. I didn't know what that had to do with our previous night's ambush, but there must have been some kind of connection, because he was saying something about killing the blankety-blank enemy over and over again.

Wow! He was mad about something and I had set him off! Maybe he didn't like me after all, or maybe he'd just had a bad night, too.

When I was at Fort Polk and had not yet realized the proper procedure in addressing an officer, I made the mistake of hollering, "Hey, you!" when I needed someone to give me a hand.

A lieutenant had responded to my request, along with informing me of his rank. No big deal. However, he soon called the company together in formation and had us stand at attention. He ordered me to report to him in front of the 140 men.

As I stood at attention, he informed the entire company of the error of my ways. Then he began a lecture, using army nomenclature, directed at me. He stormed up and down in front of me, waving his arms and yelling how he had a clear understanding of how polluted my parents' gene pool was, and how there had certainly been incest in my family. Next, he hollered about my low IQ and shared his personal knowledge that even my brothers were illegitimate.

He maintained his inspirational talk for quite some time and just about wore himself out imparting his knowledge of profanity. I kept his admonitions in mind after I was ordered to return to the formation. I must admit it had been quite a revelation to understand how important second lieutenants thought they were.

Lt. John wasn't a bad guy, even though he was saying derogatory things about my family and me. He was just a little more eager and "gung ho" than I was, that's all. One thing I did know about him: if there was going to be a fight, he would be there with us. I wouldn't have to worry about getting support the way I had when I was a kid.

BOOM!

There was a HUGE explosion.

Big chunks of dirt and rock rained down on us.

I thought I knew where the blast had come from and took advantage of a good chance to get away from the lieutenant so he could think about our suggestions.

David and I ran around the boulder and looked for Bozo. He was still where we had seen him standing, but was now lying on the ground with a dazed look on his face. I looked to the left and saw a hole about eight feet in diameter and six feet deep.

Looking back over at Bozo, I couldn't believe he was alive. The lieutenant, David, and I had been protected somewhat by the large granite boulder, but he hadn't. Rex said that when he heard the blast, he looked over and saw Bozo hovering horizontal in the air before falling to the ground.

After the commotion died down, the platoon sergeant told me he had stepped on a booby trap the night before and the ground gave way under his foot. He thought for sure when he moved his foot he would be dead, but it didn't go off.

That incident must have brought the cardboard-covered booby trap to Bozo's attention, and for some reason he decided to fool around with it. The only thing protecting him was that the booby trap must have been set too deep in the ground, blowing most of the charge upward in the air. It seemed like a miracle he wasn't hurt and it was amazing he could still hear.

This was a true example of "a fool rushing in where angels fear to tread."[2]

10

INTERROGATION

By the time I saw the prisoners they were blindfolded, hands tied behind their backs, sitting on the ground about four or five feet apart, and facing away from each other.

Three of our guys, checking an area, had come across a small cave that was slightly concealed. Two VC were hiding inside wearing only dirty white shorts and smelling of urine. They weren't armed, so there hadn't been a big problem capturing them.

A South Vietnamese soldier had been sent out to interrogate them. He brought an old crank telephone with him. After he talked to them for a while, it was obvious he wasn't getting any information. He set the phone behind one of them. He then took two bare copper wires and connected one end of each to a hookup on the phone. He tied the other ends to the little fingers on the VC's hands.

The interrogator asked more questions, but still not getting any answers, gave the old phone a few cranks. The VC started shaking, talking, and crying. He didn't know what electricity was, which was somewhat of a surprise to me.

The two VC ended up telling where they had hidden two hand grenades. We located the grenades and the ARVN left with his prisoners.

I realized the little shock he received from that telephone was nothing compared to what the VC often put others through when torturing them in the villages.

Lying in ambush, we sometimes heard the sounds of

someone being beaten, as crying and wailing came from the village. It felt terrible, listening to cries we could do nothing to stop. The villagers sometimes had to pay with their lives when they didn't give the cruel VC thugs what they wanted.

We patrolled through the area a few more days, going into villages, searching the grass huts called "hooches" for weapons, explosives, booby traps, or tunnels, and checking out anyone or anyplace that seemed unusual.

Most hooches had a small dirt bunker either inside or just outside the entrance, where the family could take cover or hide. Every now and then a bunker led to a tunnel where the VC were hiding. If we found one and it looked suspicious, we threw a hand grenade inside. It was hot, tiring work, especially seeing as how we had to pull guard every night and an all-night ambush every third night.

I couldn't get used to being a soldier in a combat zone. We were armed to the teeth—and a danger to ourselves. Sometimes I felt confident, only to have a sniper's bullet shake me up. I wanted to be able to know if his next shot would get closer or not.

Did I have to worry about the wild shots that weren't very close as much as the ones that snapped past me? How many VC were there?

I wanted answers, but there were none to be had, and there weren't going to be any soon.

Most of the time when we were in brush or trees, if we received fire, it was over so quickly that we couldn't tell where it came from, or how many were shooting at us. The only good thing about it was that our reflexes were getting faster at hitting the dirt.

The night ambushes always scared me. I hated them because there were so many unknowns in the dark. It was easy to get lost while moving to our location for the night. When things didn't go as planned, it was confusing and hard to correct anything that went wrong. I wanted to see the enemy if he was coming, so I never went to sleep. I was one of those kids who wouldn't pull the covers over my head when I got scared at night. If something was going to get me, I wanted to see it. It was the same on a night ambush. I lay there with my eyes open all night, looking into the darkness. I needed to get used to the different sounds and smells, and to realize the enemy was troubled too. I was still learning.

We were up at dawn one morning after sleeping in the bush. The soldiers who had been out on an all-night ambush came back into camp. But there was a problem: Bozo had forgotten his hand grenades at their ambush site. Now, some of us had to hump back to find his grenades. I was given orders to be one of them.

I definitely had an attitude about going and made it clear to anyone who was or wasn't listening. It was becoming obvious we were going to have to keep an eye out for this guy as much as for the VC.

The sergeant called me on my whining. I knew he was right because I wasn't helping with a bad situation. I had to learn how to work with Bozo and be okay with it.

Was that even possible?

I needed to try. I couldn't help but think that, if he'd been dealt with back when we were lost, we wouldn't be having this problem now.

11

DEATH'S STING

We had been in the area for several weeks and had checked out most of the villages, so we received orders to head back to base camp. After arriving at LZ Bronco, we headed for the mountains to the west toward Laos, with fully loaded rucksacks. The mountains went up to an elevation of 5,000 feet and were covered with jungle. At night, with three layers of green canopy over us, I couldn't see my hand when I touched my face. Even in the daytime, the layers of tree branches overhead made it darker than usual. It was so thick that we wouldn't be able to clear a landing area for our supply choppers to get down if we needed them.

We now had been in-country for only a little over a month. It was our first time going to the mountains and we didn't know what to expect, but we knew we were more likely to find the NVA there. We walked most of the day in the heat and set up our perimeter the first night in the foothills.

We learned early on that when we looked for Charlie all day, it was much too tiring to dig a foxhole and pull guard, only to take off early in the morning and do it all over again. We were too beat. However, if we suspected trouble, it would be worth digging in for the night. That night we were unsure of our surroundings, so we all dug foxholes just in case.

Our platoon worked up and down the mountains for several days. Sometimes we found a trail and walked on it for a while. One trail had trees on both sides with the bark rubbed off up to about six or seven feet high. We found large heaps of dung piled up three feet high next to the trail. Something *really* big had been here.

Surprisingly, while moving through the jungle one day, we ran into Rusty's platoon. I hadn't seen my California friend much since we'd left Hawaii. It was kind of amazing to come across him way out in the middle of nowhere. We reminisced about our time spent together at Fort Polk and how much we enjoyed the humidity. We talked so long we didn't notice our platoons had moved out without us. I, for one, moved very quickly to catch up. Being lost once was more than enough.

The platoon wasn't very far ahead of me. We made it through the thick jungle and came out into an open brushy area and headed down toward a creek. As we made our way down the hill, we saw a clearing in the brush and a hole in the ground. The hole was about two feet in diameter and appeared to go down about 18 feet before getting a little wider at the bottom. Someone dropped a grenade into it. Lt. John said he wanted the hole checked out after lunch. He sent a squad-sized patrol out along the creek to check for NVA; then we broke for lunch.

While we were still eating, I noticed David, the guy with the starlight scope, heading over to the hole. Since he was one of the soldiers who had recently found the VC in a cave, maybe he wanted to find a cache of weapons and ammo, or perhaps he thought it was a spider hole that was used by VC snipers.

After a few of us finished lunch, we went to see how David was doing. He had lowered himself into the hole with a small cord. We gathered at the opening to wait.

"Hey buddy, are you about done down there?" someone hollered into the darkness.

"I don't have any strength; I can't pull myself up!" he called out weakly.

He must have passed out then; we couldn't get another response.

We immediately started looking around for rope and

realized we didn't have any. We were getting very concerned and grabbed the only thing we had to use, our pistol belts and the slings on our rifles. We rapidly stripped the gear off of the belts and fastened them together the best we could. Don, who was close to David and had been with him at the cave when the VC were discovered, quickly sat down so we could tie one end of the belts around his ankles. He then rolled over headfirst into the dark hole. We held the belts and let him down.

I didn't know Don well, but found out later he grew up in a mining family in Tennessee. At the time I was amazed at his lack of hesitation heading into the inky blackness.

Soon we could hear his muffled voice.

"I have him! Get us up!"

Three or four of us began quickly pulling hand over hand. Finally Don's feet appeared at the top of the opening.

We had them!

I was touching Don's boot with my fingertips, but as we grabbed for him, the pistol belts and slings broke apart and both men fell to the bottom of the hole with a thud.

The lieutenant got on the radio and called for a chopper to come out with a long rope. Word came back that it would take two hours before the chopper could arrive, so we set up a perimeter and waited.

The patrol that had been sent out earlier came back in and said they had spotted NVA down along the creek. Things were starting to stack up against us.

As we sat, a loud shrill scream came from the top of the high hill we had come down. It didn't sound human—it sounded weird and unearthly.

Was that what rubbed the bark off those trees and left huge dung piles?

I was already shook-up. This day wasn't going well.

It seemed like forever before the chopper arrived. When it did, it centered over the hole about 25 feet up, dropped down a rope, and hovered there. The rope was quickly tied to another soldier's ankles, and he was lowered into the hole. Dust and debris were blowing all over the place and we feverishly worked to retrieve our guys. As Don was pulled up to the waiting chopper, he slowly rose past us, feet-first.

"Lordy, Lordy, Lordy," the sarge heard him say; but to those of us watching, he looked unconscious.

Next, David, throwing up, was pulled up and out of the hole.

As soon as the men who had been in the hole were on board the chopper, it headed away and quickly disappeared behind a hill.

It was hard to tell exactly what condition David and Don were in, but we had high hopes for them. This bad situation could get worse. All the noise and commotion from the hovering Huey and our rescue efforts had made us vulnerable. If Charlie was watching, it wouldn't be long before he took advantage of our chaos.

Hours later, word came over the radio and spread through the platoon that both David and Don were dead. The news affected me in ways I would never understand. I felt like someone had reached inside me and ripped my heart out.

Death's sting caught me off guard as the reality of what had happened hit me. We had been so close to saving them—even touching Don—when the belt buckle broke with that terrible snapping sound. The sight of our arms and hands stretching out, frantically grabbing, as we helplessly watched David and Don fall back down that dark hole wouldn't leave me.

I wanted to go away somewhere—to hide from everyone, but that luxury was not to be had because of the danger of being in enemy territory.

I had high respect for the courage those guys showed going down after David. I didn't know how the others felt, and I didn't ask. It was too overwhelming for me to talk about.

In the morning we got word there had been a mistake and Don wasn't dead, but was in bad shape. This news helped me feel a little better, but that inner ache was still there. Soon orders came for us to move out.

It didn't make sense to me. I wondered how anybody could ask me to continue to fight a war when I hurt so badly. I was learning the fact that war had nothing to do with feelings, and that I had better start changing how I dealt with them. That was when I began forcing my feelings as far away as possible. I couldn't make good decisions or function well if my feelings lived too near the surface.

12

AMBUSHED

With heavy hearts, we loaded our rucksacks on our backs and started back up the hill the same way we had come. We eventually learned what had happened with Don. He had been pronounced dead after he was taken off the medevac chopper, toe-tagged, and put in a body bag. While he was being wheeled away to the morgue, for some reason, perhaps to double-check his dog tags, the body bag was reopened. He made some slight movement and was checked again. They discovered he was alive. He was sent to Japan for a while before going back to the States. He had become blind, but thankfully it was only temporary. He never went back to combat duty.

The jungle was hot and humid, and it was a real workout packing weapons and gear to climb up, up, up a mountain, only to go down, down, down and then back up again. We climbed through the mountains and ended up farther in the jungle, still looking for the North Vietnamese Army.

The NVA wanted to fight only on their terms, when they really believed they could take us. This often meant that we had unknowingly taken on an overwhelming NVA force. This time, however, word was that we were to meet up with the rest of the company and become part of a big blocking force so we could get a large unit of NVA surrounded. Then they would have to fight us because there would be no other way they could avoid being encircled.

We found our company deep in the jungle-covered mountains back toward Laos. Once there, we settled in for the night by setting up our part of the large perimeter, and started pulling guard. Again, the jungle was so dark I could touch my face without being able to see my fingers. In the morning we saw a squad of guys headed down the mountain to fill canteens with water from a creek far below. Ben, a rifleman from First Platoon, and I were lucky enough to talk one of them into filling our canteens for us while we waited up on the mountain.

I had gotten to know Ben earlier in Hawaii. He was one of those fellas everyone loved. He played football at home and was very strong. Once, after mail call, I saw him with a pile of opened letters from home. Most of them had a picture of a beautiful girl inside.

Wow! How did he pull off getting so much fan mail?

Really, there was no trick to it. Everyone liked him. He had red hair and freckles and loved to have a great time. He also enjoyed winning.

We were both in a good mood that day. After all, we had just finagled a water delivery at a time when water was hard to come by.

While we waited, we talked. One of the things he mentioned surprised me.

"I am really excited about tomorrow," he said.

"Why on earth for?" I wanted to know.

"Because I can hardly stand waiting until we catch up with the NVA," he answered. "I want in on the fight! I am ready to take them on!"

He seemed to have no fear. I wasn't like that at all and the possibility of a big gun fight worried me a lot.

It wasn't that I was afraid of guns. As kids, my friends and I had plenty of them. One of the ways we hunted rabbits when we were old enough to drive was by sitting on the front fender of a car. Two of us would be out on the fenders while someone drove along a dirt road in the country. If a rabbit got up, we were ready to start shooting. Sometimes it got a little wild when the rabbit sped up and the driver gassed the old '54 Ford, especially if the fender paint had been waxed recently. Rabbits were good at making sharp, high-speed turns. When that happened, the driver hit the brakes and turned. Often doing 30 to 40 miles an hour, we went flying off the fender, rolling onto the dirt, gun and all. I knew what some people thought, but we'd shot a lot of rabbits that way. It had been boring in the little podunk town where I grew up, so we stayed busy doing crazy stuff.

Just after I turned 18, one of my buddies and I bought ourselves pistols and drove out to the country to try out our new guns. It only took about a half hour before I'd shot myself in the leg. We hurried back into town to see the doc. He fixed up my leg okay and I went home. My dad had not been happy about what I'd done, but he could see that I had learned a valuable lesson about the business end of a firearm. That lesson, even learned the wrong way, had given me great respect for firearms. In Vietnam, more than anywhere, I needed that respect.

Ben and I talked for hours before the guys came back with our water. When they finally arrived, Ben went to his platoon and I headed back to mine. As it got dark, we heard heavy artillery rounds flying overhead. This continued all night long. Our firebases were shelling where they thought the NVA would be. I was worried about the next day and the possibility of my first meeting with a large enemy force.

My mother had sent me a little Bible with a metal plate inside the cover. I guess she hoped it would help stop a bullet someday. I had been reading the Psalm where King David wrote that a thousand might fall at his side and ten thousand at his right hand, but that no harm would come near him because God would protect him.[3] I read that with contempt and skepticism. To think that God would watch over us, or me, for the next few days, just seemed impossible.

In the morning, Second Platoon was sent out on patrol to see if we could locate or make contact with the NVA. Ben was walking point for First Platoon, and they headed off to an area where the mountains were high and the jungle so thick that you could hardly make your way through it. An ambush could be around any corner or right in front of you and you would never see it until it was too late.

The way we were trained to deal with an ambush was brutal. If you were ambushed and not killed or wounded too badly, you were to turn toward the enemy, fire your weapon, and walk into the oncoming bullets—shooting everyone and everything. But usually we would hit the ground and start shooting from there. If you had any brains and wanted to keep them, you learned to eat dirt fast.

In an ambush, the thing you really want to do is run away, but that's your worst choice because you're a great target to shoot in the back. Although it was horrible, facing the ambush was your best choice and had to be made instantly or you were dead. The problem was, a soldier had to be hardened with experience in order to be able to make that choice. He had to look straight at death and do something about it without hesitation.

When an ambush goes off, it's loud, fast, and confusing. With the firepower that we had, an ambush would last only seconds, with hundreds of bullets being fired. If the point man was caught in an L-shaped ambush where he was being shot at from the front and the side, his chance of getting out alive was slim to none.

Shortly after we started our patrol through the mountainous jungle, we heard the sound of automatic weapons fire from the direction First Platoon had headed. The gunfire didn't last long, but it sure sounded like contact had been made with the enemy. We continued our patrol into the afternoon and made no enemy contact.

When we returned to our company's perimeter later that day, we heard that Ben had walked into an ambush the NVA had set off and was killed instantly. The terrible news shook us all.

If someone as tough as Ben could be gone so quickly, what would the rest of us do to make it through this war?

I found a spot on the side of a small hill to sit and wait until his platoon returned. When I saw one of his buddies come walking in on the trail just below me, I called out to him.

"John, what happened?"

John was a tough guy, but when he looked up at me I saw more pain in his eyes than I had ever seen.

He didn't need to say a word.

We all had suddenly lost a wonderful friend and the meaning of war was digging painfully deeper inside all of us.

The shelling continued that night and I knew that in the morning we would be on the move again. It was very hard to put Ben's death aside and continue on. Self-pity because of what we were facing wasn't going to help. Each man had to find a way to deal with his feelings and move on. For most of us, that meant pushing them way down inside and beginning to build a hard wall of protection around them.

The war continued despite our loss. There was still a large force of enemy soldiers that needed to be dealt with sooner or later.

The next morning, Second Platoon went on patrol deeper into the mountains, headed in the same direction that the artillery had landed the night before. After winding through the jungle and mountains for several hours, we found a large NVA base camp that was well hidden under triple-canopy jungle. The camp was deserted; no one was there and it looked as though they had left only a day or two before. The camp could have housed hundreds or maybe a thousand NVA or more. There were barracks, cafeterias, and other kinds of structures, all made from natural materials found there in the jungle.

In the camp I found a backpack, filled with maps and other information, hidden in a tree. I had no idea why it had been left behind. As we kept searching throughout the camp, I found some simple drawings that had been colored in with crayons. They looked like school children had made them. Along with the drawings was a *New York Times* newspaper with the front pages showing war protests back home; in essence, supporting the very enemy that was killing us and invading the country we were here to help.

Why have we been sent here to fight and die in this war if our country back home isn't going to support us?

Regardless of what I thought, this war would continue whether these issues were worked out or not. The *Times* newspaper article reminded me of the Civil War, when newspaper propaganda was turning the public against the war effort. Union General Ulysses S. Grant knew if he didn't finish the war within a few months, the negative publicity would cause the North to lose. Now, here it was happening right before my eyes.

During our operation the NVA managed to slip away from us without much contact. The nights I had spent worrying about a big fight came to nothing. I was learning that just because I worried about something, didn't make it happen. A few nights earlier I had held God's Word in contempt for no real reason; I still needed to learn more about faith and trust before I judged it helpless in a time of fear.

13

BOOBY TRAP

First thing one morning we headed out of the LZ, through the rice paddies again, and into the villages. One of our rifle squads made contact with four VC and killed one of them. When the surviving VCs fled, our guys went after them trying to reestablish contact but couldn't.

It was extremely hot that afternoon, and we were taking a break in the shade. A small chopper landed nearby and an officer got out. I watched as he had a conversation with our officers. He threw his helmet on the ground and started yelling and swearing, waving his arms around, wanting to know why we weren't chasing down the remaining VC.

This was the same officer I had fired up in Hawaii, and he hadn't changed a bit. He was a bad piece of work. I had seen him once before in his chopper when we were under fire and a couple of rounds went his way. The next time I saw his chopper circle overhead, it was 5,000 feet higher in the sky. I had no respect for him at all.

It was obvious he couldn't care less about us and would use us in whatever way he wanted if he thought it would help him get ahead. The only thing the guy had on his mind was the enemy body count. That was all that mattered.

He left the area and we moved out to look for the long-gone VC. We searched and patrolled for some time, but didn't find anyone. We were in the enemy's backyard, and it was easy for them to stay ahead of us most of the time.

One day on our usual patrol, we were searching a village and came across two young men that were old enough to be soldiers. We took them with us and began the long walk to our firebase, heading back a different way than we had come so we wouldn't set a pattern that could be noticed and used against us. Rather than walk in the rice paddies, we took a path through small rice fields and brush which made it easier to walk, but more dangerous because of the potential for mines and booby traps.

I was at the rear of the patrol. A woman was following along behind, jabbering at us to let the men go. We hadn't been on the trail very long when I heard a loud explosion from up ahead. When I looked forward, I saw one of the Vietnamese men fly through the air and land on his feet. He tried to run away but was stopped.

As I moved toward the front of the patrol I heard someone say that Lt. John took most of the blast and his CS gas grenade had gone off, making it impossible for anyone to get near him. By the time I reached his location, the gas had dissipated and a couple of guys were there with him. I went over and knelt down next to him. There were holes all over his arms, hands, ears, face, and body. He was in a lot of pain. I tried to help him get into a position that didn't hurt so badly, but nothing worked. He had taken a lot of shrapnel. The medic checked him over, but there was little that could be done.

The point man had tripped a booby trap on the path and kept walking. The lieutenant, close behind him, unknowingly walked into the delayed blast. The point man took some shrapnel, but not as much as the lieutenant. A medevac chopper flew in, and with some pretty incredible maneuvering, landed right next to us. We quickly loaded the wounded and had them on their way to the hospital. That was the last time we saw Lt. John. We heard he was pretty bad off and was sent out of country.

Each time something like that happened, it drove home

just how dangerous it was to take each step. The constant inner nagging that the next step could be your last was always there.

It was weeks before our platoon received a new lieutenant. During that time the platoon sergeant, who we called "Papa," was in charge of our daily operations under the company commander. Papa was a good man who didn't have any grand ideas about our platoon winning the war in short order. He was "Regular Army," and followed orders well. Every one of us knew there was the "Right Way," the "Wrong Way," and the "Army Way." Papa was better than most at doing what he was told all the time. He did have moments, however, when he got fed up with the army way.

14

SOMETHING HEAVY IN THE AIR

They don't strike you when you're strong.
They strike you when the day's been long.
Now you're tired and feeling weak.
You only want to get off your feet.
Don't put down your guard. You're in their backyard.
Yes, you would like a little sleep,
but they will strike you in your need.
They're not here to help...they would like to create hell.
Bullets flying everywhere. I can't see "Charlie" anywhere.
I drop down hard to the dirt.
I am now very alert.
Look around; is anyone hurt?
Now it's quiet, they are gone. Fired all they had; then ran.
Hoped their bullets in this short time
through our flesh their way would find.
How this creates fear!
Inside of me my beating heart I hear.
Maybe I can just sleep right down here.

We were still in the lowlands, working the area and looking for VC on our daily patrols from the firebase. One morning we assembled with First Platoon next to the barbed-wire gate where we would leave the base perimeter. Standing in front of me was a soldier named Niles, who I had visited with a few times but didn't really know. He was carrying an M60 machine gun for First Platoon that day and I could see four hand grenades hanging on him, as well as 200 rounds of .30 caliber ammo draped over his shoulders.

It was one of those rare times when I felt I was supposed to know something, and that feeling wouldn't leave me. When I looked at Niles, I felt like I was supposed to tell him something, but I didn't know what. It was strange, to say the least.

Soon after that we all moved out, First Platoon headed west, and we headed east through rice paddies toward a village. It was really hot that day and we were traveling light—no rucksacks—just guns, rockets, grenades, ammo, and canteens, along with some C-ration cans stuffed in our pockets. By this time the guns and other things were nothing but tools.

Before I was drafted I'd liked guns; they fascinated me. Now we carried them everywhere. They were there when we ate, sat, walked, pooped, and slept. We had to clean them, take care of them, and know where they were at all times. If I didn't have one near me, it felt as though something was missing.

It was difficult walking through the muddy paddies. It seemed like our feet were always wet and it was tough to keep them from rotting. It was hard to come by enough time to remove our boots and let our feet dry out. We worked our way slowly through the water, sometimes walking on the dikes. We were always worried about dikes being booby-trapped, but after you were hot, soaked with sweat, and tired from slogging through the mud, fatigue affected your judgment. When this happened, we might be willing to take a little risk we ordinarily wouldn't, and walk on a dike for a while.

When we made it to the village, we began our routine: searching through everything, checking out the people, looking for VC and supplies. Most of the time we couldn't find anything and that day was no different.

As we left, we headed off through one of the small gardens and I noticed some green peppers growing. I thought they might spice up my C-rations, so I picked a couple of them and put them in my shirt pocket for later.

We moved through a sandy area with some trees off to one side. Bullets started cracking past me and I dove to the ground, trying to figure out where they were coming from. The shooting didn't last long; there were maybe 20 rounds from an automatic weapon. We waited a short time and then got back up.

This kind of thing happened every now and then. Most of the time a VC would be hiding in a well-camouflaged spider hole, sometimes a hundred yards away. He would pop out of it and fire off a quick burst of gunfire at us. Then he would drop down the hole, pulling the camouflaged lid over his head, and we would never find him. It was frustrating, but that was all part of our day.

We started off again, trudging through what was becoming sandier terrain as we neared the beach. I felt my chest starting to burn, but didn't think much of it. As time went on, the burning still hadn't gone away; it just kept getting hotter and hotter. Finally, I couldn't take it any longer so I stopped and opened my dirty smelly shirt to take a look. My chest had a huge red welt on it! When I dove for the ground under fire earlier, I had crushed the hell-hot peppers and now it felt like they were eating through my chest. I was on fire!

Not much else happened on the patrol, so we moved on back to the firebase. When we arrived, we learned that First Platoon had run into bad trouble. Their point man, Chuck, had taken a bullet through his right leg, which permanently paralyzed the lower part of his leg and foot. Niles had stepped on a mine and the explosion set off the grenades he was carrying. He was killed instantly and two other soldiers were wounded. It was a harsh day for First Platoon.

When these things happened there wasn't much said. We just tried to get it together and move on. I never understood why I had those incomplete impressions about Niles that morning.

But there definitely had been something heavy in the air.

15

BOYS TO MEN

We moved out early one morning from LZ Bronco and headed south down Highway One. After traveling about a mile, we came upon a red and yellow mini-van that had driven over a land mine the VC must have buried in the road the night before. The van had been blown off the road and into a rice field about 30 feet away. All the windows and the undercarriage were blown away and it looked like the shell of some big dead bug lying out there in the field. About a dozen Vietnamese men and women had been killed and someone had laid their bodies along the side of the road before we arrived.

The people killed that day were never removed from the roadside. We passed by them several times that year and their clothed bones were always there.

Why didn't anyone move or bury them?

This was so different than what it would be like back home, but we were half a world away from there.

Wasn't there anybody who cared about those people? Didn't they have families or loved ones who wanted to know where they were?

We also came across a dead VC soldier lying alongside one of the trails we frequently used, and his decomposing body had remained there the entire time as well.

As we passed by those bodies over that extended period of time, I adjusted to the fact that we were surrounded by death all the time. I was left with the impression that life was cheap and nobody cared about what happened to anyone else. That really affected me and made me guard against having compassionate feelings.

Our platoon kept moving on patrol through rice paddies and villages. We were searching for VC or anything out of the ordinary, but hadn't found a thing. Around noon we took a break for lunch.

The platoon was strung out in a long line sitting on a well-traveled path about five feet wide. There was no one around but us. The weather here was hotter and more humid than in the mountains. The trees behind gave us some shade. Out in front the area was more open. There were some large stacks of straw about 75 to 100 yards away, and hedgerows and rice paddies in the distance.

I was sitting on the path near the end of the line and used a P38 can-opener to open my lunch of beans and franks. No juicy hamburger, fries, and ice-cold Coke today. I was drinking warm rice paddy water from my canteen, flavored with an iodine pill to kill all the little germs—a taste one doesn't forget.

While I was gobbling down my beans, I saw an older man out in front of me, dressed in black pajama-like clothing, and a broad cone-shaped hat. He kept looking at us from behind a pile of straw. He would step out from behind the pile, stare at us, and then step back. He did this about four times over a period of three or four minutes. About the time I wondered what he was up to…

BOOM!

There was a huge explosion.

Dirt fell from the sky, getting all over our lousy food. I thought for sure someone had been killed or badly hurt from the blast. I wasn't sure exactly what had happened, so I got up and headed toward the action about 90 feet away.

When I got close, I could see an enormous hole about seven feet across and six feet deep in the middle of the trail. Ace, a railroad worker from Pennsylvania, was sitting next to the hole on one side with a stunned look on his face, and Fred, a mechanic from Oregon, was on the other side, sitting half-propped on one arm, with his free hand covering one ear. They weren't moving and had hardly come to their senses.

It was shocking. I couldn't believe they were alive. We always did our best not to bunch up next to each other when we were on patrol or taking a break. They had been sitting far enough apart to avoid being blown to pieces.

"Whoa, that was a close one," I said.

Ace had a dazed look on his face.

"Yeah!" he mumbled.

I was amazed he could hear anything or answer me.

Fred shook his head slowly.

"I thought that old guy was acting suspicious, so I rolled over to get my rifle," he said.

That action had probably saved him when the blast went off.

I couldn't see the old man anymore, but I was sure he had detonated the booby trap. At the time I saw him repeatedly looking at us, the thought didn't enter my mind that he was trying to see if our guys were close enough to set it off.

When I came to Vietnam I had no opinion of the people who lived here, but that was changing. I was angry and trying to come to terms with what had just happened. I was getting my fill of things looking different than what they really were. What my eyes saw could be so deceptive.

How was I going to tell who was who?

Most everyone I saw looked the same. We were told that we wouldn't be able to tell the VC from the villagers during our training, and here it had almost killed us.

I was learning the hard lesson of not trusting the apparent, but had no idea the price that would be paid later for making a mistake because of a situation like this.

Despite the uncertainty of our surroundings, we got ourselves together and continued searching the area for the rest of the day.

Papa decided we would pull two ambushes that night. At dusk we split into two groups. One group went to set up an ambush near the area where the booby trap had been set off, and the other headed to the beach area where NVA were known to work out of small boats at night. I was with that group, and as soon as it was dark we headed for the beach. We were walking on a wide path in the dark and were making good progress when we heard an explosion far behind us.

Soon word came over the radio that a grenade had been thrown in the middle of the other ambush, wounding several guys, and they needed our help. We started back at a rapid pace, but didn't know where they were located. It was really dark and we couldn't see much. We started moving across a small open area as we got near to what we thought was their location.

Unfortunately, what little communication we had established over the radio failed. I heard a shot; then rifles and a machine gun opened up, sending tracers and bullets right at us. I dove for the ground while tracer rounds snapped between my legs and under me as I hit the dirt. These bullets were way too close and I tried to become one with the earth. In the confusion, one of us got a round off with the M79 grenade launcher.

BOOM!

After it hit we heard shouting in English. We realized the guys we were coming to support had mistaken us for the enemy and opened fire. We started yelling at them and the shooting stopped. The M79 round had landed on them and now more had been wounded. Ace was among the eight injured, but no one critically. We got together and began patching them up. Soon we had a Medevac on the way.

While we were waiting for the chopper, one of the wounded was moaning a little too loudly for my comfort level. I moved over to him, bumped him with my boot, and asked if he could hold it down some. He had taken quite a blast from both explosions and had some shrapnel in his arm. I assured him he wasn't hit too badly. This made him feel a little better and he was able to quiet down. This was pretty scary stuff, being 10,000 miles away from home, in the middle of the night, in a country where most people had it in for you. Heck, I was scared, and I wasn't wounded or lying on the ground from a concussion.

Once again, it was a real wonder we hadn't killed some of our own guys. Our lack of combat experience was showing. I never thought war would be like this. I hadn't realized that there would be so many costly mistakes and bad surprises.

We knew we were in the enemy's backyard, but never realized how hard it would be to find him. It was nerve-wracking to be constantly looking for Charlie without success. This was his terrain, his familiar territory. He had grown up in these rice paddies, hedgerows, and mountains, and always seemed to know where we were. His booby traps and land mines were deadly, and he had plenty of time to set them up for us and then hide in the shadows while we struggled.

How could we get a handle on things in such a tough situation and make it through this?

The constant uncertainty of our surroundings, the death and serious injury of our guys, and the elusiveness of the enemy was taking a toll on all of us. We were making many mistakes that could cost us our lives.

Even though I was very scared most of the time, I thought I was tough enough to handle whatever came my way. I hadn't realized yet that things were always going to go wrong. When they did, we needed to make adjustments to improve the situation and keep moving toward our objective. No touchy-feely stuff, no matter how bad it got.

I needed to learn how to look at what was happening and make it black or white; to quickly come to the most important decision first, then act, right or wrong. I hated this. I preferred to take time to make decisions. It was maddening to be rushed when some of these choices would have such deadly, life-changing consequences. I could easily do the wrong thing and someone would die, or I would get myself killed in no time. I didn't have enough knowledge yet. I just needed to stay alive long enough to get it.

Growing up had been easy and fun. I'd managed to get through the few minor problems I had, with good advice from those around me when I needed it. In my family, we loved each other, and I had lots of friends. I wasn't a drinker and was able to stay out of most trouble even when we'd done crazy things—like for excitement, my friends and I took turns sitting on the bridge over an irrigation canal, wearing water skis, and holding onto a rope tied to the rear bumper of Davis' '54 Ford. He gave it the gas and jerked us off the bridge onto the water and away we went.

Wahoo!

All we had to do was lean away from the speeding car above us on the dirt canal road and hang on. His old green hot-rod had no problem getting up to 70 miles an hour with dust billowing up behind it.

For 16 and 18-year-old boys, it had been wild and only cost us gas money. One of my older friends had warned me we were crazy and could get killed because the water was like concrete at that speed, the canal was narrow, and it would only take one wrong move to hit the water or dirt sidewall. None of us thought we would get hurt or killed, though. Life was simple, easy, and fun.

Now, just a few short years later, and all had changed. Now I was faced with problems that gave older men a struggle, much less 20-year-old boys. What a learning curve! Our time in-country had steadily become worse. We were being forced to change and I wasn't sure if it was good or not. We were losing our boyish attitudes. Tenderness was fading away as we came to grips with this deadly job.

The medevac chopper got there sometime later. We put the wounded on it and away it went up into the night. I wished I was going with them, back somewhere safe, maybe to a nice bed where someone else would pull guard while I slept. I was dreaming. Now that we had the wounded on the chopper, the rest of us headed back for the beach.

Everyone seemed to be on edge as we moved along the trail in the dark. We had been going all day and half the night in this mosquito-infested country, and now it was the middle of the night and we were tired. We came to a village and walked through the edge of it. I cared less and less for the people in these villages all the time. Right or wrong, I blamed them for the constant danger we were in when working the flatland.

I thought it must have been really easy to recruit new VC. The young boys had to be bored and tired of bending over all day to either plant rice or harvest it in the heat and bugs. There wasn't much to do in the local village: no electricity, no TV, no radio, no sports, no cars, no money.

Then along comes Charlie VC, telling stories about the "Bad Americans" and how to kill them.

"Here, kid, this is a hand grenade. Just pull this and throw it at them; and don't forget to run away really fast."

"Just put these two wires on this old battery when you see an American near that tree. Don't forget to run, they may not be too happy. If you're good, I'll try to get you one of these neat rifles. Wow, won't you be cool?"

I knew that some of the villagers believed the VC's lies and worked with them to kill us. If the village leader didn't buy into his schemes, Charlie gave a demonstration of what would happen if he didn't go along with the plan. He either got with the program or would get beaten or killed. The villagers were always under pressure from someone trying to force them to comply. It was easy to see stress on the older faces, the look of despair. No matter what happened, they would end up the losers. All they could do was wait out this war.

We continued on our way to the beach along the dark path. After moving a half-mile, I saw a frail old man standing outside his hooch. He became frightened when he saw us and started shaking and chattering to himself with his hand over his mouth.

Suddenly the soldier several feet in front of me slammed the butt of his rifle into the old man's head, knocking him back toward the hooch. It shocked me. This was uncalled for and cruel. Here we were, armed to the teeth, walking next to the man's village in the dark, and frightening him. Then this big guy busts him hard with the butt of his rifle. I was very unhappy with the villagers, but being mean to a frightened old man wasn't right.

Frank was walking behind me and saw our guy hit the old man too. We never forgot this cruel act and kept a watchful eye on this member of our ranks from then on. He was a bully and a coward when he hit the old man and would show his cowardice again later. He was the only soldier I ever saw turn tail and run when it took everything a man had in order to stand and fight during a real battle.

We kept moving toward the beach. We got there at dawn as three small boats were moving out to sea. That was against a curfew that had been set to keep the NVA soldiers from using boats to move around. We called out for the occupants to stop, but they kept moving farther out. Papa gave us orders to open fire and we did. By then they were about 400 yards away so we put several hundred rounds on them.

Someone in one of the boats called out and headed back toward us, but the other two boats kept moving out to sea and were soon out of our range. The boat that came to shore had a lone man in it. He had been shot under his left arm and the bullet exited under his shoulder blade. He was in surprisingly good shape and hadn't lost much blood. The medic started patching him up as he was being questioned. He gave no answer as to why he didn't return at first or who or what was in the other boats. We called in another medevac chopper and soon he was on his way to a hospital. We headed back to our firebase, hopefully for a little snooze before we would be sent out again.

16

NO FUN

For the next few weeks, we worked through the villages and rice paddies nearest LZ Bronco. During the day it was monotonous, dangerous work patrolling the area. It was boring to keep patrolling the villages and searching the hooches in the heat and humidity. There were mosquitoes buzzing around us day and night, looking for blood.

The rice paddies were breeding grounds for hordes of them and they didn't have any trouble finding us. We were warm blooded, hot, and sweaty, with shirt sleeves rolled up and open collars. Someone in our company was always coming down with malaria. We were given little pink pills to take every day, but they gave some guys the runs, so they wouldn't take them. Even if you took your pills, and I did, there was no guarantee you wouldn't get sick. The mosquitoes never let up. We needed insect repellent as badly as bullets and reeked of its smell. I kept it handy with three or four small plastic squirt-bottles, hidden away in the endless pockets on my jungle fatigues.

We didn't get baths or clean clothes but every 45 to 50 days. Once, at night, I put my head on my arm to go to sleep and it stunk so badly I had to move my head to keep from choking. When we took a bath, it was in a small creek or pond, with heavily armed men standing guard while we nervously soaped off in our birthday suits. And there were insects even worse than mosquitoes. If we went barefoot to let our feet dry out, screwworms came up through our feet and ended up in our stomachs. The remedy for that was no fun. If you got them, and were lucky enough to convince the lieutenant that you were really sick, you would go to the rear. There they would try to put you on KP or bunker guard while you waited to see the medic. It was a lose/lose situation.

When you finally got to see him, the doc would give you a large pill. I mean that sucker was huge. After you choked it down, you were instructed to eat no food for two days so the worms would eat the pill, and then you were sent back to the field. When the worms were ready to come out, the "no fun" got worse. Most times, when you had the urge to take a crap, it was already too late; and we had no clean clothes to change into.

Eddie, a Southern California boy, had his own way of viewing our harsh situations. Not only did he make us laugh, but sometimes gave us pause. Frank related Eddie's insight while pulling late-night guard with him after our company had lost a couple of our guys.

Frank: "Eddie, it sure is getting rough here."

Eddie: "Hell, man, this ain't nothin'. Now, growin' up in Watts during the riots was some screwed-up bad shit."

Eddie was a real stand-up guy who could be counted on in tough situations. He had a way of putting things into perspective.

Eddie and Joe were different as night and day, yet were best of friends and hung together. I didn't know Joe well, but he had kept his cool while we were lost, and I had a high regard for that.

One morning, we broke into platoons and went out searching the area. We started drawing machine-gun fire from a hooch a little over 500 yards away. The captain was nearby and called in some artillery rounds on the enemy's position.

We were given orders to send a rifle squad into the area to check it out. There was some discussion about whether this was a trap set up to get us to send men over there, but the order stood. Eddie, Joe, Bruce, and some others were sent to check out the area.

The squad had a ways to go and the guys were walking on a grassy slope next to the rice paddies. I was behind a small dirt rise and couldn't see them. When they had gone about 200 yards, there was a loud explosion followed by a terrible scream that none of us will ever forget.

Eddie had been toward the front of the patrol and stepped on a Bouncing Betty, right after a couple of guys had unknowingly walked past it.

Bruce was one of them. When he heard the scream, he turned and ran back to where Eddie lay in the wet rice paddy.

Eddie was conscious, but in really bad shape. Both of his legs and an arm were almost blown off, and he had other injuries. Bruce did his best to hold him out of the water, trying hard to help and encourage him.

A medevac chopper was called in, and the guys did what they could to patch Eddie up while they waited. He was soon on his way to the rear. The rest of the day was a blur. We changed course and never made it to the enemy's position.

In the evening, we returned to base. Late that night the word spread that Eddie had died. We were sure going to miss him. Joe was crushed and I doubt if he ever got over the loss. This had been another brutal lesson that came at a deadly price.

17

ERROR'S LOSS

Shortly after Eddie was killed, our company was sent north to a place called Tam Ky where there was always trouble. The enemy had a lot of support in this area, and we had to keep our eyes open. We patrolled the area daily, going through rice paddies, hedgerows, and trees. We stayed in the field and set out ambushes every night, waiting for Charlie. We all hated ambush duty for a lot of reasons. It was always dangerous because we could just as easily end up the ones being ambushed.

Usually six to eight of us would get together at dusk with grenades, Claymores, M16s, a couple hundred rounds of ammo each, and maybe an M60 machine gun. No overnight pack. We moved out to find our pre-determined site and lay hidden in bushes or anything that would give us cover. We had to maintain complete silence during the long night. Besides being scared, it was hard to keep yourself awake the whole time. We had been humping all day and were tired. Some nights, rain would pour down on us.

Night or day we had concerns. This was a dangerous area and we needed to be on our toes. On one of our patrols, the company was strung out in a long line, walking on a narrow dirt path through some trees. It was my day to carry the machine gun and I held it in front of me with its strap over my shoulder and across my back as I walked along.

The area looked pleasant and the green leafy branches of the trees hung over the path covering us with shade. It was midmorning and not very hot. We hadn't seen anyone or been through any villages yet. We got off to a good start through the area and it almost seemed peaceful. We kept traveling along the trail for another half mile or so, and then stopped for a short break. I leaned back against a tree to take some of the weight off the heavy rucksack on my back.

I noticed movement about 130 yards away, across the rice paddies, where brush was growing high. Someone looked out from behind one of the trees growing out of the brush and then ducked back behind it. He did this several times and that nervous feeling began in the pit of my stomach. It was hard to make out who it was or what he was up to.

Concerned that someone was going to detonate a land mine on us again, I sent a message up the line saying I thought I should fire into the area to ward off any trouble. Word came back to fire. I set the M60 on the path with the front bipods holding the barrel off the ground. Dropping my pack, I lay down behind the gun, pulled the stock into my shoulder, and fired four bursts of six rounds into the direction of the movement. Jumping up, I grabbed the gun and moved out with Jerry and a squad of men, running across the watery paddies to check out the area.

When we arrived behind the trees, we found a level area covered with large flat stones. It looked similar to a patio without any cover. I looked about ten feet away to one side and saw a small boy who looked to be about eight, wearing only a pair of shorts, lying flat on his back, his arms spread out.

One of our guys was already kneeling next to him, as blood flowed into a large puddle on the stones underneath his body. The soldier was on the radio, giving information about the boy, who had been killed by a bullet that went through his heart.

Away from the boy, standing beside some trees, was an older woman wearing a worn pale orange dress. She was holding her hand to her face, with five or six children standing close around her. All of them were sobbing.

My mind would not let me see the horror on their faces.

Time froze—it was all so wrong. But there it was, right there in front of me: blood and sorrow. My soul was now tainted and it wasn't well. All logic failed, just as these words fail now. The brutality of what had happened forced itself on me and I couldn't think about it. The boy was gone. Only tragedy was left, and I was a big part of it.

Ode to the Woman in the Orange Dress

Still I see her standing there
with that lost and painful stare!
Error's loss has bestowed a guilty wound
that logic cannot heal.
Hidden away on the heart never to be removed.
Love has taken a bitter blow.
Oh, what can heal?
Yet it is only Love which can heal unforeseen sorrows
at its risk.
The reason to step through Love's gate?
It sees pain and cares.
'Tis the salve that heals hidden wounds.[4]

18

REPATRIATION

Numerous villages were scattered throughout the flat rice paddy area where we were working. The villages were made up of five to ten hooches made from tree limbs covered with dried rice stalks. Most hooches were small, with door-less entries and no windows.

The only furnishings were a low table the family squatted around to eat, and a small wood-burning stove made from mud or clay along an inside wall. Rarely, there would be a small cane or bamboo bed.

The mama-san of the family spent hours working around the little stove, keeping it heated just right with wood she had stacked in the corner. She might have a pot and pan with black burnt bottoms stacked next to the stove or hanging above it.

The dirt floor appeared to be swept clean. The mama-san usually held a small child as she worked, and there were always plenty of children around playing some kind of game.

Most villages had a hand-dug well for drinking water. There were trees growing throughout the village and around the outside edge, providing lots of shade. The villages were built up a couple of feet higher than the surrounding rice paddies, with small bushes making hedgerows around the outside edge. When it rained, the water would drain from the higher ground down into the paddies.

The VC controlled many of the villages in the area. Some villagers were willing participants, but others were coerced and mistreated so the VC could take the rice and other supplies they needed.

In order to deprive the VC of this support, there was a plan called Repatriation which came with orders to go into the villages to relocate the occupants and their belongings.

During this operation, when we found a store of rice, we loaded it onto choppers and sent it to a storage area for the villagers. Then we gathered up the people, caught what animals we could, and loaded them all on choppers to go to a new place where they would live and farm. When they were gone, the village was set on fire and we shot the pigs and chickens we were unable to round up.

Of course, the people feared this for many reasons and didn't want to leave, but that didn't matter. The plan moved forward regardless of their feelings. It was easy for the villagers to see us coming across the open fields long before we arrived, and we would often hear a warning gong being sounded when we were spotted from afar. Many times, while headed to the villages, we were met with sniper fire. When we arrived, we usually only found old folks and mana-sans with children. Anyone we found between the ages of 12 and 60 were considered suspect.

Most mornings we made the long, hot trek out of Bronco's perimeter, through the rice paddies, into a village, then started the relocation. After spending a long, hot day loading rice, crying women, and children to be relocated, we didn't always return to the firebase at night. Instead we set up some kind of ambush. We would then go back to the firebase the following morning.

Our ambushes were seldom set off because the enemy didn't show up. Yet we had to keep at it for months at a time before the higher-ups decided we were getting worn out. Sometimes we would set one man to watch the trail and the rest would sleep lightly. I couldn't sleep while I was on ambush. I felt that too many things could go wrong, and I really wanted to see the bad guys if they came.

Repatriation was a miserable job—but then, all of our jobs were miserable. No matter the assignment, there was always a catch. We didn't get to guard sandy beaches with pretty girls lying around on them. We didn't get to guard the freezers containing ice cream. I don't think there were any good jobs in the infantry.

19

THE LITTLE MESSENGER

There was a sense of urgency in her childish voice as she tried hard to communicate with us.

"Baby-san, dee-dee-mao! Baby-san, dee-dee-mao!"

We were sitting beside a village close to the sea when a little girl, who looked no older than six, walked up to a small group of us and repeated the words to us over and over again. She really wanted us to understand. We figured out that she was saying all the children were leaving the village. We looked at each other.

Uh-oh.

If the children were leaving, we knew something we wouldn't enjoy was about to take place.

We had arrived earlier in the evening after we left a different village area where we had been looking for hidden VC supplies all day. It was dusk, and Gary, the Third Squad leader, was sitting with us. Tall and savvy, he was a preacher's kid from the Midwest. He and Jerry were cutting up and exchanging smart remarks as the platoon waited in our pre-ambush site. We always went to a pre-site first to lead the enemy to believe that was where we were setting up. As darkness fell, we would move to the actual ambush site.

We looked around and saw that the whole village was, in fact, leaving. It was obvious something was about to go down. Gary grasped the seriousness of what was about to happen. He moved over to Papa and informed him of the situation. It was almost dark as Papa gave orders to move out quickly. We were to stay low and head down the beach to a patch of trees about 500 yards away. Most of the men had no idea why we were moving out in such an urgent manner.

We had just arrived at the clump of trees and begun spreading out when the location where we had been sitting minutes earlier erupted with multiple explosions. Automatic weapons fire completely raked the area and seemed to go on forever. If we had still been there, our entire platoon could have been wiped out.

I didn't realize it then, but we had just missed the "big one" we had always heard about and dreaded. It was unbelievable we had escaped, but we weren't out of trouble.

The clump of trees we were hiding in was about 25 yards in diameter. We had recently been assigned a forward artillery observer, or "FO," with no experience. These guys were trained to call in coordinates for locations needing artillery, and were sent out to the field as needed. Papa was standing with him on the other side of the trees. They had a map and a red-lens flashlight, trying to figure out where we were so they could call in artillery.

I really wanted that flashlight off. The VC must have realized we had gotten away by now, and I was sure they were furious they had missed us. Charlie opened up with recon fire, shooting in all directions, in an effort to get us to return fire so they could see our muzzle flash in the dark and locate us.

I was lying on the sand, getting a Claymore ready to put out in front of me, when the recon fire came snapping in rapid succession through the trees. One of the soldiers standing nearby called down to me.

"Hey Bob, what's that snapping sound?"

I couldn't believe my ears. We had drawn plenty of gunfire since we had been in-country, and he didn't know what that snapping sound was? Where had he been? I looked up at him.

"If you don't get down, Fruitcake, you're going to find out what that snapping sound is."

He could tell I wasn't joking and fell to the sand immediately.

We were in big trouble if they found us. The water was only about 50 yards behind us; I could hear the waves washing in on the sand. We couldn't escape that way if we were discovered. We could easily be out-numbered, surrounded, mortared, and overrun with an assault. By this time, the FO was trying to call in artillery on the site where we had been. We could hear it coming but it was off target and hit around 1,500 yards in the opposite direction. One thing for sure, our FO needed more practice.

We set up three-man positions all around inside the trees where we were hiding. Papa sent the new FO over to my position for the night, and I already had the guy that didn't know what the snapping sound was. I didn't trust either one of them. It was going to be a long night, so after a while I told them I would pull an hour of watch and then the two of them could pull a half-hour together. They were okay with that and asleep in no time. I was pretty shaken up by what was going on and didn't see how they could just pass out like that.

We were still getting a little recon fire. I believed Charlie really wanted a piece of us that night, if he could just find us. Our defensive position was poor at best. The moon was out so we could see, but so could Charlie. We had to keep our movement down. After an hour, I woke the two of them to pull the next half-hour's watch together.

I kept my eye on them for about 15 minutes and they both fell asleep. That was all I needed. I let them sleep and stayed awake through the night. Around 0200 hours, a dog from one of the nearby villages came to our small perimeter and began to bark at us. It stayed just out of reach and barked most of the night. We tried to grab it, but it managed to stay out of our grasp. If we could have caught it, I have no doubt it would have been pulled apart in seconds without a sound.

Lying there, pulling guard that night, I felt that our odds in this country weren't good, and seemed to be getting worse every day. On our first night in the field, one of our own had been killed with friendly fire; on my first ambush, I had a grenade go off in front of me, cutting my face; I was in the hospital when it was mortared, killing many inside and out; one of our own had become lost and was found, dead, the next day, his body splayed out on a bridge; David had died in a tunnel; Ben was killed on point; Lt. John had been blown up; Eddie died after stepping on a mine; and we had just missed being killed in an ambush.

What if more of our guys got killed?

The fear of the unknown was heavy on me, a young, inexperienced soldier. Whether in broad daylight or the darkness of night, there were the constant dangers of stepping on mines, tripping booby traps, or being shot by snipers. I was exhausted from a continuous lack of sleep and the heavy pressure of the terrible dangers of war. I felt very inadequate for the tasks that lay before me. I knew I wasn't the only one feeling the pressure of adjusting to these fears. We were all trying to stand tall despite the danger, but the weight of it was showing on our countenances. Sometimes the weariness from shouldering the load showed up in carelessness, which, in doing dumb things just to relieve the pressure, might result in getting you wounded or killed.

The Bible says "Without a vision, the people perish."[5] I was losing the vision for my future. I began to feel a great distance from the future I had always taken for granted. Going home, getting married, and having a life away from the war might not happen. Right here and now—this was my future.

At dawn we started moving out right away. We had made it through the night, but that didn't mean this was over yet. We were still miles from our firebase.

We worked our way through villages and hedgerows until we came to the rice paddies. Out in front of us I could see as much as 4,000 yards of open rice paddies flooded with six inches of water. This would be the best place for Charlie to try to get a piece of us if he was ready and had a mind to do it. We had moved out early enough that morning, and made good time getting to this location, so Charlie would have to be "Johnny on the spot" if he wanted to get much of a shot at us. He would also have to guess where we would be heading out into the open.

We split into two groups and spread apart with about 40 yards between us. We headed out into the paddies, and with every step in the water, our boots sank right down into five inches of mud. When we had gone so far that we couldn't run back for cover, the VC opened up with two automatic weapons.

The group I was with started firing back into the hedgerow as we dropped down into the muddy paddy. We had to put enough fire on Charlie so he would have to keep his head down. The other group of guys ran like crazy until our rifles were empty. Then they started firing as they dropped down. We jumped up and started running, reloading as we ran, until we heard their rifles empty. Then it was our turn to shoot as we dropped back down.

We did this back and forth until we worked ourselves out of range and Charlie stopped shooting at us. The tactic worked.

Running in wet paddies is a real chore, but if bullets are chasing you, you're highly motivated. We were a tired, muddy mess, but none of us had been hit.

20

BACK TO THE BEACH

It was amazing that we had made it through the ambush across the rice paddies without any casualties, but I was too worn out to think about it—or to be thankful. We still had several miles to go before reaching base camp.

When we finally arrived, we rested up for a few hours at our newly-assigned bunkers along the perimeter where we were to pull guard that night. Then we received orders that we would be heading back to the beach in the morning. After our near-miss experience in the village and our muddy 400-yard dash, I was not looking forward to going back.

Being in Charlie's backyard had many disadvantages. The VC's efforts to kill us were spoiled solely by that little girl's simple warning. The thought of going back to the beach terrified me and I felt desperate. We had become the hunted, not the hunters.

With all that had happened in barely two months, I had run out of faith that many of us would make it through another ten. I had a little hope, but not much.

Three years before I was drafted, I had wanted to go on a youth mission to another country. After I signed up for the program, I received books to read about people who had done some great things by having faith in God. These people were Christians, and the books were based on the Bible. After studying them, I had learned there was good reason to build my faith in God and have confidence in the abilities He had given me.

I felt ready to go on the mission, but when it was time to

leave, my appendix went bad. I needed an operation and wasn't able to go.

I had still gained valuable information to build on, such as, "Faith is the substance of things hoped for, the evidence of things unseen," "...the just shall live by faith..." and "...we walk by faith, not by sight."[6] I hadn't realized at the time that reading a book with good stuff in it was one thing, but living it was going to require help.

What someone really believes often becomes evident under extreme pressure. A guy from another platoon made some claims about his faith. He left me with the impression he could just tell God what he wanted, and everything would come about to his liking. But, as pressures set in on him, his behavior changed. He took to drinking and smoking, and started swearing. It seemed he had given up on his faith to the point he no longer believed it.

Now it was my turn. Everything about my faith was on trial. The pressure was on in a very deadly way. The situation looked bad and I was having a very hard time being hopeful about the future. I was running out of inner strength and needed help. When it got dark, I pulled the first hour of my guard. Then I went inside an empty bunker where I could be alone.

Growing up, I had learned from my father that we could come to God with our requests. I had also learned from watching him that a believer's prayer was powerful. My father had grown up in rural Texas. There were 13 children in his family and he was the third youngest. He was born with his left leg one-and-a-half inches shorter than the other and so had to wear one shoe with a built-up sole. He had a bad back because of this and was always in pain. When he was about eight, his father died. His oldest brother, even though he was blind, became head of the house and made sure everyone did their part. They were a poor family and worked as farm laborers picking cotton and other crops to survive during the Great Depression.

His mom saw to it that everyone went to church on Sundays. The family trusted in God during those hard years and the knowledge of God was instilled in my father. He had become a Christian during his early twenties, and took advantage of the power and simplicity of prayer. Growing up under his roof, I had heard his heart-felt prayers often. They were said with quiet fervor and such feeling that it made a big impression on me.

As a young boy I had accepted that Jesus was God's Son[7] and asked Him to forgive my sins. Since then, a hunger had been growing inside me to learn more about who God was.

I enjoyed reading the book of Proverbs in the Old Testament of the Bible. It gave good instructions for how to live and make good choices. It said to get wisdom and understanding, that they were better than gold and silver.[8] I had started praying about life and where I fit in. I wanted to do what would please God and still have a real life full of fun and adventure. But I wanted life with meaning, not religious acting.

I admired Jesus. He set an example for me with how He cared for people. He stood up and showed this care for them in many ways, like healing and forgiving them, even facing death for them on the cross and not running from it.

I knew about facing death now, and it was scary.

I was in a tough situation. I felt desperate and in need of help that I believed only God could give. I believed Jesus was who He said, but did that mean He would always hear my requests?[9] I decided to ask, hoping that He would.[10] It's not like I had anything to offer Him. Besides, what could God need?

I looked rough, smelled bad, and was dirty; so the only thing I could bring to the table was an honest heart and the belief He was a loving God. He knew my mistakes and there were plenty of them. He knew the pain and fear I felt, even some I'd caused and the guilt and remorse that it had produced, so there weren't any hidden secrets. I believed God was powerful enough to create this world like the Bible said, so anything was possible.

Feeling hopeless, I knelt on the dirt floor of the bunker, raised my hands above my head, and looked into the darkness.

"Jesus, I'm in bigger trouble than I've ever been before and I really need some help here. We all need Your help. Would You please protect the guys in my platoon and not let any more of them be killed? I don't care so much if we get shot up, just no more dying, please. I will pray for each man by name every night, no matter what's going on. And, just one other little thing: do we have to go back to the beach?"

That was all I had in me. I was finished. It felt like I was talking to the sandbag ceiling and thin air. No voice answered saying everything would work out. I was simply kneeling there, saying a desperate prayer.

In the morning, we got new orders to pack up and be ready to head for the mountains.

Did I hear that right? The mountains? Had my request that we not go back to the beach been heard?

I felt renewed hope as we packed up. On our way out of the firebase, we walked past a 175mm artillery piece on tracks. After we passed it about a hundred yards, I was caught off guard when...

BOOM!

It fired right over our heads. It scared me half to death. The blast shook me inside and out, physically and mentally. I got the feeling that I shouldn't get over-confident, and our hard times were a long way from being over.

21

ORDERS

I had been drafted in June of 1967 and soon learned I didn't care much for the Army. Someone was always giving me orders to do things that I didn't want to do. I had never done well being ordered around. As a teenager, I had gotten myself into fistfights because other guys wanted to push their weight around and tell me I had to do what they demanded. This never went over well, especially when coming from someone who was full of himself, or in my opinion, not using his brain. To me, this meant most of the people in the Army.

In basic training at Fort Lewis, our drill sergeant had given us a spiel about buying U.S. savings bonds, but told us it wasn't required.

I was the only guy in the platoon that hadn't bought a savings bond, so the sergeant wasn't happy with me. There was some kind of incentive for him to get all of his troops to buy bonds. He woke me up several times in the middle of the night by either dumping my footlocker out on the floor or throwing everything out of my wall locker. After the third time, I'd had enough.

"Why are you *doing* this, Sarge?" I asked.

He ripped into me about not buying a U.S. savings bond.

"We're gonna talk about this later, soldier," he informed me. "Come to my room after chow!"

I showed up.

"Whitworth, why haven't you bought a bond?" he asked.

Then, without waiting for my reply, he proceeded to tell me why it was important for me to do so.

I was really mad about the way he had been trying to make his point.

"I don't *want* to buy a bond, I don't *have* to buy a bond, and I'm not *gonna* buy a bond! You told us we didn't have to buy one!"

The discussion was over. I guess he'd just wanted to be sure I didn't want any bonds.

He hadn't dumped my locker again. End of subject. That was, until basic training was almost done.

One of the last exercises we had to complete was the "live-fire" course. We were marched out to the shooting range wearing full gear: our pack, entrenching tool, canteen, gas mask, and rifle. Gray smoke flowed over us as we low-crawled on the dirt under barbed-wire fences. Machine guns fired live bullets just over our heads.

After we finished the exercise, the sergeant marched us off the course and instructed us to form a single line standing about five feet apart. He ordered us to knock out a hundred push-ups, just so we wouldn't get cocky about living through the machine-gun fire. While we were pumping out the push-ups, he put someone else in charge and disappeared. I was at one end of the long line of troops and was almost done, breathing heavily. I turned my head.

Holy mackerel!

The drill sergeant was running toward me wearing a gas mask and carrying a long stick with a tear gas grenade taped to the end. He shoved the gas-spewing grenade under my face as I drew in a breath; then ran down the line of troops, tear gas flowing into our lungs as we gasped for air.

I rolled over, desperately trying to get my gas mask out of its pouch. My eyes and nose were on fire and I could feel a churning deep down in my stomach that was going to come up. I ripped the cover open and jerked out the mask. My eyes were closed in an effort to keep the gas from burning them. I jumped to my feet, trying to pull the mask over my head with all the little tangled rubber straps tugging through my hair. I pulled on the bottom of the mask and forced it against my face. I took a deep breath in an effort to seal the mask, but more gas flowed in through the unsealed sides. My stomach let loose and I barfed out the bottom of the mask as I pulled it away from my face. I tried again, jamming the mask back on my face and sucking in a stronger breath. The mask sealed this time and I began to breathe more easily.

I looked at the guy standing next to me with his mask on, but couldn't see his eyes through the big plastic lens because his mask was completely filled with puke. The soldier next to him turned and ran, but he couldn't see where he was going. He ran full speed into a large pine tree, hit his head, and fell to the ground. It was mass confusion, with most of the troops on the ground throwing up. The drill sergeant was laughing. He had gotten his final revenge.

That sounds bad, but the first time I ran into real unchecked power in the Army was after basic, during AIT in "Tiger Land" at Fort Polk. We'd spent days wandering through the swamps and slogging through muddy water while playing army games. I don't think there was a better place to train for the jungles of Vietnam than the swamps of Louisiana. They trained us to read a compass in order to find certain locations in the night by following a compass course for a certain time and distance.

Then it was time to go through the "escape and evasion" course. The company was called together and told where the course boundaries were. We were ordered that under no circumstances could we go outside those boundaries. We were going to be trucked out to the beginning of the course late that night and make our way through the swampy jungle to the finish line without being caught by the so-called "enemy troops." If we were captured, we were to go with them peacefully. We would be taken to the enemy's compound and coerced to give information. We were instructed not to give anything other than our name, rank, and serial number.

After dark, truckloads of us had been taken out to the start of the course and dropped off. We split up into small groups and began working our way through the course. When we were crossing a road, a truck pulled up quickly. The "enemy" jumped out and grabbed some of our guys. The now-smaller group I was in disappeared quietly into the night.

We were lost part of the time, but came across another road, figured out where we were, and proceeded. We moved through brush, trees, and vines for a while until we saw a light in front of us. As we got closer, we could hear the loud screams of men. It sounded like we were nearing the gates of hell. We moved closer yet and I heard men being tortured. That didn't sound good, so I decided it was time to cheat.

I wasn't the only one who'd come to that quick conclusion. Together we made our way to the boundary line and crossed over into "out of bounds." We ran until we saw the end of the course, ducked back inside the boundary, and crossed over to "safe" ground. I caught a truck back to my barracks and hit the sack for the night.

In the morning, after breakfast, the company was brought together and seated in a large room. A sergeant stood up in front of us. "I was the commander of the enemy compound last night," he boasted.

He swaggered around as he continued. "I pried information out of everyone that was captured."

He then began to share some of his methods with us.

"I had a burlap sack put over the prisoners and then had them hung upside down and beaten. If they still wouldn't talk, I had water poured into their noses while they were hanging there. That cracked almost everyone."

He continued to swagger back and forth in front of us as he spoke.

"I made them cuss their folks and tell me juicy information about their wives or girlfriends," he laughed. "It didn't take long to make them tell me anything and everything I wanted to know!"

Finished with his bragging, he ordered three soldiers in the room to stand at attention in front of the company.

"Each of these men cracked," he bragged as he gestured toward the three. All of them had bruised and swollen cuts across their upper lips, just under their noses, and across part of their cheeks. I could tell they were in pain.

"These were the toughest of the bunch," he stated.

He pointed to one of the soldiers and said, "That one was the least tough—the easiest of these three to break." He motioned to the next soldier. "This guy was tougher, but he gave in too—after a bit more persuasion," he said with a smirk.

He put is hand on the shoulder of the third soldier. "Then there was this guy. He was a hard one to crack and lasted longer than anyone."

The commander/sergeant stepped back and motioned to the three soldiers. "I ordered these men held to the floor while a wire was stretched across their faces, under their noses, and down the sides of their cheeks." He motioned across his own face. "Then I slowly had more and more pressure applied to the wire, until it cut into them. That finally got 'em talking."

I wasn't sure what this sadist had wanted us to get from his torture lesson, but I'd drawn my own conclusion:

Think for yourself no matter what anyone says.

The next time I ran into the misuse of power in the Army, when the orders had been just too wrong to obey, happened in-country. Our company was working its way out of the mountains. It was going to be days before we reached our main firebase. We had been on patrol all day in the jungle.

Late in the afternoon, we came down the hill at one end of a small valley and walked along the inside edge toward its small mouth at the far end. The valley was about 900 yards long and maybe 400 yards wide. As we moved along, we could hear the NVA on the sloping sides, digging in their positions for the night. We couldn't see them in the dense jungle, but there was no mistaking who it was and that there were plenty of them.

Once my platoon reached the mouth, we began setting up for the night. First and Third Platoons were on their way to our location as well, and when they arrived, about an hour before dark, they busied themselves setting up their night defensive positions.

By this time we had received our replacement lieutenant, Lt. Dennis. He had transferred into the Army from another branch of the Armed Services. He was a very young-looking man who had no lack of confidence.

I noticed that a short distance from me, our captain, known as "Six," was brainstorming with all the platoon lieutenants. They were having a hot discussion about the orders they had been given. Those orders were that our company was to set up in the middle of the valley for the night. When the NVA attacked, artillery would be called in all around us to destroy the enemy.

There were no defensive positions in the valley; it was wide open with no cover. The NVA were on the higher ground. There would hardly be time to dig in for the night. We would be sitting ducks. If the valley opening were closed off, we could easily be surrounded, heavily mortared, overrun, and wiped out.

The officers rightly knew we wouldn't be able to make it through the night, but the upper echelon was willing to use us as bait and sacrifice us, with the hope of getting an NVA body count. The bad feeling I had about that senior officer when I'd shot him with blanks in Hawaii, had sadly proved to be true. The order was insane! I overheard one of the lieutenants suggest to the captain that he forward the information that two of the platoons weren't going to be arriving until after dark. I never learned what information was relayed, but our company didn't move into the open valley.

The lieutenants did, however, send out two ambushes. Third Platoon sent guys on an ambush back into the valley. Six guys in Second Platoon, including Rex and me, were chosen to go out through the mouth opening into the rice paddies and set up an ambush to protect the entrance to the valley. When it was dark, the six of us headed out about 500 yards into the paddies where we lay down behind an 18-inch dike for cover. It was hardly a hiding place to set up an ambush. I had been in some lousy sites before, but none this open. We carefully set out Claymores in front of our position. In addition to the mines, we all had grenades and M16s.

There was a full moon that night, and if we sat up or moved around, we could have been spotted. It was wide open for thousands of yards in front of us. To one side, about 20 feet away, the ground started gradually sloping up to a hill that was about 100 feet high. There was scraggly brush scattered over it. The path we were next to headed up this hill. If Charlie came from that direction, he would spot us from the high ground and our ambush would backfire.

We knew the real reason we were sent out there was to be an early warning for the company. The NVA would run into us first and it wouldn't take much to blow us off the face of the earth. We had no foxholes and no sandbags, only the small dirt berm to lie beside for cover. If anything did happen, we would be lucky if we had enough time to radio back to the company before we were dead.

Around 0100 hours, Rex came up with the idea we should just blow our Claymores and throw our grenades. Then we could radio in that we had set off our ambush and needed to come back into the company perimeter. We needed to figure out how to get out of this position, and were quick to believe his idea might work. Lying there in the darkness, knowing there was a large force of NVA nearby, made a guy think that being anywhere else had to be better than where we were.

Heck, what could go wrong?

So, tired, scared, and stupid, we blew the mines and threw our grenades.

There are times when you do what you think is a good idea, but as soon as you commit, you know you've made a mistake.

What if they order us to stay put?

My belly tightened. It was a little late for common sense. We had just blown off most of our defensive power, and, if anybody was watching, exposed our position for sure. Of course, like every night, I had already made my request that God would keep us from dying. But now I had the thought that He might be looking down on us, laughing at the lame-brained thing we had just done. Thankfully, I remembered that His Word says in Hebrews that He sympathizes with our weaknesses.[11]

We radioed the company that we had blown our ambush and couldn't find any bodies so we were headed back to the perimeter.

"Negative! Stay where you are!" the order came back.

After that stupid stunt, I could do nothing but push my face down into the dirt and try to be one with the earth. That was one long, nerve-wracking, sleepless night, but nothing else happened.

In the morning, we headed back to the company. When we got there, the other ambush patrol had also just returned and there was a big argument going on. The night before, Third Platoon had sent a six-man ambush out into the small valley. The sergeant in charge led the men to the location where the ground started up the mountain. It was the place we heard the NVA digging in earlier. He ordered the squad to head up the hillside into the dark jungle, toward the NVA's perimeter. At that point there was a consensus.

"You're an idiot, Sarge, and you can take your order and shove it where the sun don't shine!"

The whole squad agreed he was a fool and refused to follow his direct order. The ambush had been set up somewhere else. Now, within the company perimeter, the sergeant was furious and wanted Six to discipline the men. The sarge and the squad were cussing each other and ready for a knock-down drag-out fight.

I knew that sergeant. He was a short man with an inferiority complex. He didn't have any more experience than the men in his squad. He was what we called a "Lifer," but had never shown good leadership skills. He was pompous, used bad judgment, and took unnecessary risks. He had no respect for danger. Once again, it was a case of the "fool that goes where angels fear to tread."

The captain listened to both sides and had heard enough. He looked at the sergeant.

"Drop it!" he ordered.

It was over. I was relieved to see that the captain had his number. If he didn't come to his senses soon, that sergeant would find himself in more trouble than he could get out of. His ego had a tendency to get ahead of his discretion and as things turned out, that was exactly what happened.

I knew the guys who confronted the sarge and, more than once, witnessed their true grit. I was very thankful that Six and the lieutenants were looking out for us. If they hadn't been, I'd hate to think what could have happened. I saw and understood that, with one exception, we had good leadership in the field with us.

After our dumb stunt last night, why hadn't the enemy at least probed our perimeter or dropped in some mortar rounds on us—and why hadn't artilery been called in regardless of where we were set up?

I knew what artilery could do and it would have put a world of hurt on the NVA forces.

Hours later we headed out, moving down to lower country. I was surprised that we had no encounters while we were in that valley. I was very happy and a little more hopeful for the future as we all walked out of there alive.

22

LEECHES

Huey gun-ships plastered the surrounding area with rockets and machine-gun fire as another chopper swooped down and laid a heavy smoke screen between us and the outlying terrain. We jumped off our choppers into the tall grass. With so much supporting firepower, we all hit the ground running for cover, just in case this LZ was as hot as they were treating it.

Choppers had airlifted our company to a grassy knoll, surrounded by trees and bushes, in the low mountains. As we fanned out, I realized somebody really believed we were going to be in on something deadly. Fortunately for us, the LZ wasn't hot and we were soon headed deeper into the bush.

Lt. Dennis had been with us awhile now. He gave us orders to fall in behind another platoon and after an hour or so gunfire erupted up ahead. The lead platoon had come in contact with an enemy forward observation post and killed four NVA. That meant there was a larger enemy force in the area. We were in a very dangerous place and my gut was really nervous.

Crap! I hate that feeling.

We kept moving until dusk without any other contact, and set up for the night in the middle of an area full of tall brush. It was a dark, eerie place. I had been in-country for about four months at this point, yet something about that night felt different. Yes, it was dark and we were in a scary-looking place, and I felt fear most of the time in situations like this. But this time, I couldn't get over the feeling that this place was not only dangerous, but also evil. Was it death I was sensing so near to us, or was it overwhelming fear?

I spent extra time that night asking God to look after us, and the night passed without any problems. Early in the morning we were ordered to saddle up and get on our way. No one told us why, but the whole company quickly took off on a forced march out of the area. Our platoon was the last one leaving and I was with the machine-gun crew at the very end of the long line.

Earlier that year, when we had been deep in the jungle, some of our troops had been sent out on a patrol. When they returned, they found inch-long, brownish, worm-like creatures attached all over their bodies, sucking blood seemingly right through their skin. After the worms were removed, the spots where they had been continued to ooze blood.

Yuck!

It was really messy. The guys looked like some shaking nervous drunk had just cut them all over their bodies while trying to shave them with an extra-sharp razor. They were a real sight, with pieces of toilet paper blotting the bloody spots.

Those leeches gave me a sleazy feeling just looking at them. Someone said they were land leeches. I hadn't known there were such things, but there they were, and there were millions of them deeper in the jungle. I couldn't see any eyes on them, but they could sure detect us within ten feet.

They'd stand straight up on their bottom end, and wave their bodies around in the air. Once they sensed us, they would start their humpy-looking crawl as fast as they could go, as if we were their last meal. They headed straight for anyone in their detection range. They would then work their way up our boots to our legs and usually stop there. About six of them would congregate on a small spot, and suck blood until either we noticed them, or they were full and dropped off.

Those awful little creatures were thin like a twig when empty. They were very tough before they filled up with blood, and were seemingly impossible to kill. Even when we stomped on them, they didn't seem to notice. Some of the smokers burned them with the tips of their cigarettes. Those of us who didn't smoke discovered we could dissolve them with insect repellent.

When we took a break, we sat on our helmets so they couldn't get to us. At night though, we had no defense when we lay down to sleep. When we woke up, we'd find them on the tender parts of our bodies.

Many mornings I woke up to find them on my lip, eyelid, armpit, or other unhappy spot. When they were filled with blood they had a bluish tint, and were fat and soft. Sometimes when I woke up, before I opened my eyes, I'd reach up and rub my eyelid, only to rub against a full leech. The pressure would burst it, and my stolen blood got smeared across my forehead.

Good Morning!

On our forced march out of the bush, I noticed the guy behind me had a strange look on his face, so I dropped back behind him, next to Frank, to see what was wrong. It was this fellow's day to carry the machine gun and he had the strap slung over his shoulder and back, with the 23-pound gun hanging in front of his body. He was carrying his heavy rucksack and smoking a cigarette. He wasn't tall, and took short quick steps, moving at a rapid pace.

Frank and I watched as he struggled to undo the fly on his pants and pull out the stem end of his bladder.

There, on the end, was one of those leeches!

I've got to watch this!

We were in serious need of a good laugh.

The poor guy couldn't stop walking or he would be left behind in no time, which would be dangerous, and there was no way he was going to ask Frank or me for help. That was good.

He started puffing real hard on his cigarette and when it was glowing red-hot on the end, he pulled on the stem end of his bladder with one hand until it was where he could almost see the leech. Then he reached over the bulky machine gun with the cigarette in his other hand. He could hardly walk in this position, but he was going to try to burn the leech so it would drop off. His aim was bad, and he burned himself instead.

He jumped up, jerking the cigarette away, swearing, and moaning. I had been waiting for that moment and could see the pain in his eyes, but I couldn't help myself and busted out laughing.

It took several more times of burning himself, jumping, swearing, and moaning before he finally got the mean stubborn leech to drop off.

Needless to say, he wasn't very happy with his painful, recently-burned appendage. But Frank and I were laughing so hard we had tears in our eyes and could hardly see where we were going. We weren't helping much, and that poor guy just might have shot us if he thought it would have helped his situation. Heck, I got a free show that I would have given a week's pay to see!

23

AFTERMATH

"Don't stop the flares! Don't stop the flares! Please, don't stop the flares!"

It was night, and amid gunfire and other screaming voices, the terrified plea was shrieking from the radio receiver. Our RTO, sitting in the center of our perimeter, was monitoring a battle that was taking place where our company had just come from on this forced march; that place where evil seemed to lurk.

The soldier on the radio was urgently demanding that the artillery's guns keep firing night flares over their position. They were under heavy attack and I could hear the fear in his voice. I could barely endure the frightening sounds of the battle without being able to do something.

Thankfully, we soon moved out from that position and headed back toward LZ Bronco. We set up one midmorning alongside a river. The view was beautiful, looking out across the water to the high lush green mountains on the other side.

That afternoon, an NVA soldier came walking out of the mountains and into the water, heading toward us carrying a hand grenade. He waded closer and closer until one of our machine guns opened up on him. He didn't seem to notice he was a target. He just kept coming closer. He was dead in no time and his body was pulled out of the water. We had been searching all through the mountains for the NVA with no success, and here this guy just comes out alone, crossing the river to meet us with a grenade.

What's going on inside his head?

He must have been crazy, because what he did made no sense. Maybe he had gotten a "Dear John" letter from home and decided to go out in a blaze of glory.

After a few more days of searching for Charlie and making no contact, we started moving down out of the mountains and back to the firebase. Weeks later, when we got back to LZ Bronco, I met up with Rusty. Since both of our companies worked out of Bronco, he and I got to see each other every once in a while.

"Hey Bob!" he said, "You're looking a little rough around the edges. I could smell you guys coming in a mile out."

"Why, thank you, Rusty!" I replied, "You sure are good at pointing out the obvious, Butthead."

We sat down and visited awhile before he confided in me.

"We were out on a patrol recently," he said, "and I went into a village by myself to refill my canteen with water. After I filled it, I saw a gook, dressed in black, heading out of the village. When I called for him to stop, he pulled out a pistol and shot at me as he ran away. I returned fire and we had a short running shoot-out before I shot and killed him. Some of the guys I had been with heard the shooting and came into the village looking for me," he went on. "When we found his body, he was carrying a satchel with some plans and information inside. It turned out he was a VC general, and the plans he was carrying were to wipe out LZ Bronco."

I listened in amazement. The documents in the satchel ended up preventing our main firebase from being attacked and overrun. Rusty was awarded a medal and given a week's leave out of country.

Unfortunately, while he was away, Rusty's rifle company had been in a bad firefight. Only one member of his squad had survived. I didn't realize it at the time, but the voices I had heard coming over the radio that night in the jungle were those of Rusty's company, his buddies. Losing them had been very hard on him and affected him deeply.

Those screaming voices still linger in my mind.

24

SHAMMING

We were always on the move.

Occasionally we were flown to our destination on several Hueys or one large Chinook helicopter with huge rotor-blades on each end. Most of the time though, we waded through the rice paddies, heading from our firebase near the coast into the outlying areas, regardless of what the weather was like. We walked to and from the mountains bordering Cambodia and Laos, and sometimes beyond.

We worked all the time. The higher-ups wanted us out there looking for Charlie and his supplies. If we were sent to a firebase for rest, we still pulled daily patrols and night ambushes, and then had to pull guard for their artillery at night.

We were young and could take it, but were always looking for opportunities to "sham" and get out of the field for a short break. We grunts would resort to almost anything to get back to the rear.

One time, as our platoon was on patrol along a riverbank, we bunched up close together as we walked. That wasn't smart. To one side, about 40 feet away, stood a dirt bank about four feet high with trees along it. All at once, automatic weapons fire started ripping through us. I glanced toward the bank and saw four VC blazing away with AK47s. It happened so fast that we hardly had time to drop to the ground. As quickly as it started, it was over.

That brought swear words to my lips and made me want to thank Jesus the ambush had failed, all at the same time. The shots came so close that I was checking my clothes for bullet holes! The VC had dumped 120 rounds of .30 caliber bullets into the bunch of us and disappeared as quickly as they had appeared. It was as if it had never happened! Not one of us had been hit, but I wouldn't have been surprised if there was a little doo-doo in some of our britches.

It was a strong reminder of what happened when we got lax. We joked a little about the ambush, what lousy shots the gooks were—like maybe they needed to wear glasses to help them see us better when they were trying to kill us. We simply needed something to break up the grave reality of what had just happened.

We kept moving in the stifling heat. After a while we took a break. I sat down on my insect-repellent-soaked helmet. Just as I pulled my canteen out and downed a few swallows of polluted iodine-water, the order came down the line of men:

"Move out!"

I stood up, grabbed my helmet and put it on my head. As I started walking, a huge red ant, three-quarters-of-an-inch long, crawled out of my helmet liner, crossed my forehead and onto my eyelid. Before I could reach up to brush it away, it bit me.

"Owww! Owww!" I hollered. "Darn it!"

I stood there rubbing my eye for a couple of minutes, and then realized I was all alone. I had to get moving or be left behind. It wouldn't pay to lag along behind the platoon, rubbing my eye. I had no interest in having another encounter with Charlie, and he was probably still nearby. I caught up with the guys. Hours later, we joined the rest of the company and found a place to set up our perimeter for the night.

Every night in the field we chose our defensive position, determined where its weaknesses were, and tried to somehow cover them. Then our FO would call in spotter rounds of 105mm artillery to specific positions within 100 yards of the corners of our perimeter. We did this so we could call in artillery to these precise locations if Charlie tried to overrun us.

It was always wild waiting for the artillery to hit. We could hear it coming from a mile away. The screaming sounds got louder and louder as the shells got closer. Sometimes I thought they were going to land right on top of us, especially if we knew the enemy was nearby, because then the artillery would be called in even closer. Most of the artillery guys were good and we counted on them.

When we were away from our firebase, it was a good rule of thumb not to go outside their range of fire support. Those big guns could mean life or death for us, and Charlie hated them. If you were on the wrong end of the artillery, you would never know what hit you.

That night, after I pulled my first shift on guard and lay down, I got to scratchin' and rubbin' my eye. I realized that if I rubbed it too much, my eye might swell shut.

Oh, no!

If it did, I would have to go back to the rear for a few days to eat hot meals and take it easy. Gosh, my eye was getting so bad that I had to rub it most of the night.

Doggone it!

Sure enough, in the morning, my eye was so swollen I couldn't see out of it. My nighttime endeavors had made it very painful too, so I headed over to the captain and told him I only had one eye and was in great pain. I had high hopes he would put me on the re-supply chopper and send me to the rear for medical attention.

"No."

I didn't think he was going to say that.

I have got to stop coming up with these dumb ideas.

Wilbur, a grunt like me, came limping toward us. Overhearing our conversation, he said:

"Hell! "If they won't let a blind man go in, then a cripple like me hasn't got a chance!"

Wilbur had gotten a "Dear John" letter from home awhile

back, and he wasn't happy about it. It really hurt him that he had been dumped while he was in combat, and he talked about what he would do and say to his "Ex" when he got home.

As Wilbur turned and limped away, I couldn't help but laugh. Wilbur had said it all and he was right—he didn't have a chance. His words must have had their effect on the captain, though. Hours later when the supply chopper landed, I was told to get on board. I was headed to the rear for a few days.

Back at LZ Bronco, my eye improved rapidly. Somehow Frank had made it to the rear as well. We were eating a hot dinner in the mess hall when we heard loud screams.

"Incoming!"

A siren started blowing.

Everyone in the mess hall jumped up and ran outside to the bunkers. By that time, mortars were exploding outside, but they were still quite a way from the mess hall. Frank and I decided to take advantage of the situation.

We went back behind the counter and refilled our plates with all the good stuff we could find. I surprised myself a little by not getting up and heading for safety, but after all this time in-country, I had learned a few things. When a bullet hit 70 or 80 feet away, it wasn't personal yet. But if bullets were cracking by within a few feet, you'd better get busy real quick because someone probably had you in their sights and the next one might have your name on it. That was personal. The mortars never did get close enough to our position for us to run off and leave all that hot food.

25

GRUNTS

They could say anything they wanted. The bottom line was though—grunts were expendable.

When it came to doing the ugly, dangerous stuff or some dirty job nobody wanted, we were called. The infantry was named the "Glorious Queen of Battle," but it was all hogwash. I noticed after we gained experience, those in the rear who had never been to the field were a little wary of us, as though we could be unpredictable. They hadn't been forced to face their fears on a continual basis like we had. I didn't begrudge them that. What bothered me was that we were just used up most of the time with little consideration for what we were being ordered to do.

Every now and then, the tables got turned. During our first two months in-country, one of the sergeants in the rear who was supposed to help us get our supplies, wasn't very supportive. Our captain noticed, and soon the sergeant found himself trudging through the paddies and into the mountains with us for a few weeks. After that little "appreciation hike," he improved.

Everything an infantry soldier does is dangerous, even walking. Over time, each one of us made our own risk assessments, often depending on how tired we were and our level of experience.

Once, when we had spent over a month in the field, we walked out of the mountains and through the rice paddies to a new firebase some engineers had just finished building. It had tall wire fences around it and big, strong, brand-new bunkers.

It wasn't a very big place, but had wide-open rice paddies all around it, which gave it a good field of view. That also meant the base could be seen from a long way off.

We looked like something the dogs dragged in, but the cats wouldn't eat. We were very tired, dirty, and smelly, but for some strange reason we were given permission to stay awhile. There was a mess hall with hot food and cold milk. We had struck it rich!

The next day some of us were kicking back next to the big wire fence and a bullet came buzzing through. The new engineers got nervous and started looking for cover, but we just lay there and watched them run. An old sergeant showed up after a while, and called all his men together next to where I was sitting. He told them he knew they were nervous about the sniper's bullets that came through the compound. He motioned toward us.

"See those grunts we let in here yesterday?" he said. "Watch them. If they don't move, don't worry about what's happening, but if they start ducking and taking cover, you'd better duck and take cover too."

He was actually giving us a compliment and showing us some respect. I was a little surprised since we hadn't been shown much of that the whole time we had been in-country.

However, the engineers grew tired of us in short order. Evidently, because we drank up their cold milk and made ourselves too available to their hot chow, we were shown the front gate and sent on our way. As we left, the briefness of their hospitality made me kind of hope that in the near future that sniper might bring his rounds in a little closer to them. A few close rounds snapping past their heads might result in a little doo-doo in their britches, which in turn, just might help them miss us a little.

Another time, on a day that was well over 110 degrees, we were sent to guard a minesweeping crew while they swept a road heading west, through the flatlands, toward the mountains.

For miles the crew walked down the road with their equipment, checking for mines as a large truck followed them. We walked out in the muddy rice paddies on both sides to protect them from ambush, while they walked on the dry road. Once the road was cleared, we all stopped for a break with some of us standing watch. I was covering the flank on a rice paddy dike near a small tree to get some shade.

After the break, the minesweeping crew loaded onto the large truck and drove off, leaving us grunts to walk back in the heat.

Why weren't at least some of us allowed to ride back with them? What were we, second-class citizens?

I saw the disappointment and anger on the faces of the other men in the platoon as the crew in the truck left us behind. I'm sure I wasn't the only one on that sweaty day with unkind thoughts in my mind—like a little friendly fire directed toward their truck! The men on the truck had no idea how fortunate they were that we were disciplined and didn't give in to our urges—at least not very often.

It was going to be a long walk back, and we were still hot and tired, so we continued our break for a while. During that time, an old papa-san walked up to me and I offered him some of my C-rations.

"Number Ten! Number Ten!" He said as he shook his head and pointed at the can.

Numerically, one through ten was best to worst instead of the other way around. Number Ten was as bad as it gets.

Papa-san motioned toward some people gathered at a small grass hooch and gestured an invitation to join them for a meal. I did a double-take.

What could possibly go wrong besides them shooting me?

I figured they would rather take their chances doing that at night, and it was still daylight, so maybe I'd just be poisoned.

Why not? I was up for the risk.

I asked one of my buddies to take my place on watch and walked with the old man to his hooch.

Inside was a long table close to the ground and covered with food. There was a bowl filled with little fish, another with pork, and a third with chicken. They each had some kind of sauce mixed with it. There was a bowl of cooked green leaves, a large basket of rice, and large round rice disks that had been broken into chips. I had often seen old mama-sans making and cooking the rice disks over little dirt stoves when we looked through hooches on search-and-destroy missions.

A large Vietnamese family squatted around the low table. I did my best to squat down the way they did, but I couldn't find my balance with rifle, grenades, canteens, and the other gear I had on, so I ended up sitting on the dirt floor between them. The old mama-san served me up a large bowl of everything on the table and I ate it right down.

It turned out to be darn good vittles. They were talking and carrying on like I was one of the family, and I had no idea what they were talking about. Then the old man handed me a small glass with clear liquid in it and indicated for me to drink.

Was this the poison?

What the heck!

I swallowed it quickly.

The clear liquid burned all the way down, clearing out my pipes.

Wow!

I had not been prepared for such a good, friendly lunch and didn't know how to thank them. Even if they would be the enemy tonight, how would I know? I didn't want to wear out my welcome, so I got up and tried to thank them. The old man acknowledged my effort and indicated to me to tell my buddy to come and have some food also.

Having me come into their home, and feeding me such a tasty meal, was a kind and generous act. In a peacetime setting, it would have warmed my heart toward them, but I had already learned that even accepting acts of kindness had to be done with caution or a good time could quickly turn into a disaster.

I stepped back to the small tree and advised my buddy to head over to the hooch and get some Number One chop-chop; one of the best meals he would eat in a long time.

We had to walk four miles back to the firebase in the heat. I'd rather have had a ride in the truck, but the meal had been quite a consolation. Full and sleepy, I trudged along with the others.

Lieutenant
instructing troops
in Hawaii

Photo from Bob's 8mm

105mm
and crew

Photo from Bob's 8mm

Mmm…the
sweet aroma of
honey buckets

Photo from Ric

LZ Bronco

Photo from Bob's 8mm

Bunker at
LZ Bronco's
defensive
perimeter

Photo from Ric

175mm can
shoot 20 miles

Photo source unknown

Bob and Mama-san
with local sauce
(or something)

Photo from Bob's 8mm

Rusty
kicking back

Photo from Rusty

Beach where
we spent the
first night
in the field

Photo from Ric

Rex with our gear

Photo from Rex

Village hooches

Photo from Okie

At risk walking
the dike

Photo from Lewis

Moments before
Bob's foot was
crushed

Photo from Jerry

Bruce, Frank,
and Trox

Photo from Frank

Okie with a full pack
and grenade launcher

Photo from Okie

June 27.

Dear Dad & Mom
Just a note to say hello.
I'm doing fine. I have two $25 bonds.
I'm sending home. it seem if I keep
them I always get them wet in the
rice paddys.

Just some of what has happened today. as we
were coming in to the base comp. some
V.C. snipers started shooting at us. from
a village. Well I don't mind him shooting
so much. but when they started shooting
we all had to get down in the mud. Man
that bugs me. I thought we would get to
come all the way in without getting shot at
Or having to lay in the mud,
Well no one got hurt, Praise the Lord.

Fred just said Hello.
Well I got to go. You guys be good
and don't get into any trouble. OKAY
Take care.

                        love and prayers,
                            Bob

Letter home from Bob with note from
Fred (aka "Gramps")

Fred is going to just say hello.
I had to laugh at Bobby today because
he was laying in a rice paddy &
the leechs were swimming around him.
Well we are all fine so don't worry as
The good Lord will bring us through.

Sincerely

Fred

NORTH
VIETNAM

Demilitarized Zone
(DMZ)

Hue •

Da •
Nang

Bob's
Area of
Operation

Tam Ky •

Chu Lai •

LAOS

Duc
Pho •

CHINA

NORTH
VIETNAM

BURMA

LAOS

Gulf of
Tonkin

HAINAN

THAILAND

SOUTH
VIETNAM

CAMBODIA

Gulf of
Thailand

South China Sea

Map of Southeast Asia

Plieku •

Quy Nhon •

Cam
Rhan

CAMBODIA

SOUTH
VIETNAM

Saigon
•

Gulf of
Thailand

South China Sea

MILES   50

KILOMETERS   100

N

NORTH
VIETNAM

DMZ

Corps
Boundary

MILES   25   50
KILOMETERS   25   50   75   100

N

Hue

Bob's
Area of Operation
with approximate
locations of
Firebases

I CORPS AREA

Da Nang

Quang Nam Province

LZ Baldy
LZ Ross

Tam Ky

LZ Ryder

LZ Young

Chu Lai

LAOS

Quang Tin Province

Quang Nai
Province

LZ Cork

LZ Amy

LZ Dragon

Duc Pho

Corps
Boundary

LZ Bronco

II CORPS AREA

LZ Thunder

CAMBODIA

SOUTH
VIETNAM

Ric on patrol
along the dike

Photo from Ric

Dale getting some
rare but much-
needed sprucing up

Photo source unknown

Ace

Photo from Bruce

Bruce on
the field radio

Photo from Frank

Mini-van disaster…
aftermath of a
road mine

Photo from Bob's 8mm

Jerry crossing the
river packing the
M60 machine gun

Photo from Jerry

M72 LAW
– smoke grenade
– hand grenade

Photo from Lewis

Bob in
triple canopy

Photo from Bob

Lieutenant John
on the day of
booby-trap

Photo from Bob's 8mm

Bob with Beth on leave
between AIT and Hawaii

Photo from Bob

All in a
day's walk

Photo from Ric

Vern, Bob, and
TC shakin'
some puddin'

Photo from Bob's 8mm

Stand Down
building near Chu Lai

Photo from Bob's 8mm

Stand Down
Back: Lewis - Rex -
Jerry - Vern - Bob
Front: Steve - Bruce

Photo from Jerry

Gramps

Photo from Jerry

Sure would be fun
if we were
rabbit hunting!

Photo from Bob's 8mm

Steve
contemplating
the journey

Photo from Jerry

Landing in
Charlie's
front yard

Photo from Bob's 8mm

Track

Photo from Leroy

Air strike
near
Tam Ky

Photo from Ric

Armor
at battle
near
Tam Ky

Photo from Leroy

Portion of Frank's letter home about the battle at Tam Ky

I'll try to draw a little picture of the way it looked.

CHOPPER   NAPALM   JETS
                    BOMBS
WOOD LINE

RICE PADDIE

TANK   APC
HALF MILE

That is a little like it only there were about 10 Tanks and 35 or 40 APC's and 200 men between them. Jets all day long helicopter gun ships all day long. One jet got shot down and two helicopters. Can you immagin the noise. It was defining. Just the noise is enough to scare the heck out of you. Can you Think of it, it took us two days to get accross that rice paddie. Everytime we would get close they would open fire so heavy we would to retreat. They day we finely got into the jungle & was gunning on a APC. We were in the jungle when I got hit.

M60 machine gun and shield
on APC Track

Photo from Okie

Remembering
the fallen

Photo source unknown

Gare dining in traditional
style on C-rations

Photo from Bob

Papa *Photo source unknown*

Christmas 1968

Photo from Jerry

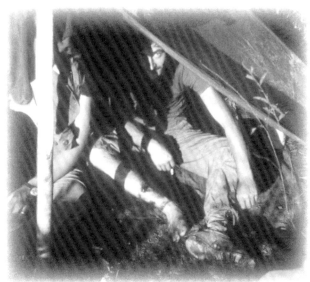

Fred with a
leech wound
on his leg

Photo from Bob

Casanova

Photo from Bob's 8mm

"Arthur Godfrey" letter to Beth written by Casanova

29 DAYS

March 12.

Dearest Bethy,
I love you.
I guess I will start
with an apology. I am very
sorry my letters have been lacking
in quantity and quality.
I have so many things
on my mind, I have neglected my
feelings toward you, which mean more
to me than anything else in the
world.
It took me seventeen months
to realize how much of the world
you mean to me. I think of you
the entire day and you fill my
dreams at night.
Sometimes I frighten my
self because my mind can take
only so much. After thinking
of my past with you for days
on end I am so homesick for
your love I can't even eat.
If the Lord gets us together again I will never let the
opportunity present itself where we
must part again. I should have
said, "When the Lord gets us together again" because a union as
perfect as ours has his blessing
and I know he is protecting our
future.

My love I cannot explain why I have difficulty in conveying my feelings for you. Maybe its because they are so tremendous, words aren't sufficient.

If I was an artist I couldn't paint my feelings for you. If I was a poet I couldn't put it in verse. I can only wait and try and prove them to you in my actions when I get home.

I wish I could offer you the moon and stars. A fine house and everything done for us so we could spend all our minutes together. We will not be rich in worldly goods but we will be rich with each others love.

Take very special care of yourself for me as I am doing the same for you. I love you so much I will think of nothing but you till we meet again.

All my love

Aurther Laffly

Wars hell baby, sorry about the wrinkles

Strolling through
the jungle

Photo from Ric

In the
midst of the
mountains

Photo from Ric

Wonderful packages
from home

Photo from Jerry

We're really short..."Tee-Tee"...almost home

Back: Bob - Gary - Jerry - Lewis
Front: Vern - Bruce - Wilbur - Fred - Steve

Photo from Frank

Jerry packing up
for home

Photo from Bruce

Bob heading home

Photo from Bruce

Back to the jungle
without us

Photo from Bruce

Reflecting on the past and contemplating the future.

Photo from Ric

Troops boarding
to go back
to the world

Photo from Bob's 8mm

26

SURPRISES

I was in the middle of getting my breakfast together when Lt. Dennis said to move out. I had been up early, digging out my breakfast: canned eggs and ham again, instant coffee all heated up with C-4, and a valuable B-3 cookie—and I wasn't ready to leave. I grabbed up my stuff as quick as I could and shoved it into the rucksack. My canteen didn't want to fit in its cover on my pistol belt, so I shoved a little harder and snapped it down. I grabbed my rifle and was ready to go.

We had spent another night in the field. A squad had been sent out to set up an ambush, but it turned out to be uneventful, which was okay with me. Now we were off again, looking for Charlie. I was at the front of the patrol when we started off. About an hour into the day, I started smelling something very foul. I didn't think much of it until the guys behind me wanted to know if I had messed my pants.

"Heck, no!"

Not that it would have been so unusual if I had, because all of us had gotten diarrhea due to bad water or a hundred other reasons. It was a frequent problem.

The more time that went by, the worse the smell became. Pretty soon no one would get near me.

"Hey, Whitworth, you smell like the walking dead. Do us all a favor and get your rotten butt to the end of the line."

OK, I could handle Frank's rejection, but now Gramps was starting in on me too.

"Don't be comin' around me, I need all the fresh air I can get in this heat."

I looked everywhere for the rotten, nasty smell that seemed to be coming from me. Before long I was pushed to the very end of the patrol.

What was this reeking, foul odor?

By that time, three hours had passed and I couldn't stand myself. I smelled as though I was decaying on the spot.

We finally took a break. I stopped alongside the path and dumped everything out of my rucksack.

Nothing rotten in there.

I checked all my pockets.

Nothing!

Everybody was keeping their distance. I was still being razzed about how rotten I was.

Thirsty, I pulled my canteen out of its cover. A blast of putrid aroma burst out! I almost yakked. When I looked inside the canteen cover, it was smeared with the guts of a flattened-out, decomposing frog!

We continued on our sweaty patrol, weaving through a dense area of brush all afternoon. I was still at the rear of the patrol, plugging along with the machine-gun crew. We were moving like a big snake, winding our way through high brush and trees. Suddenly there was an explosion up ahead. We stopped, on alert, wondering what was happening up front, when bullets started pouring past us. We instantly dropped to the path, sucking up dirt. I heard the rapid firing of M16s on full auto.

Were we being ambushed?

Bullets continually cracked about two feet over us and we tried to get even lower. It was a good thing we hadn't hesitated, or we would've been lying there, full of holes and trying to plug a leak or two.

What had they run into up there?

It didn't sound that far in front of us, but there were an awful lot of bullets coming right through where we had been standing. It was always shocking how quickly things could change. After a bit, the firing dried up and we got to our feet. I heard a commotion up ahead and soon we started moving again. I worked my way through some of the guys to see what had happened. Lying next to the path was a dead water buffalo.

It was Bozo again. He had seen the buffalo just off the path and thrown a grenade at it. Well, being fragged just ticked the big guy off, so he charged the line of soldiers. Then the shooting started. The path we were on curved back around and put us right in the line of fire. The buffalo hadn't given up easily so the barrage of bullets that didn't hit the charging animal came right into us. The men firing couldn't see us because of the high brush.

Bozo was batting a thousand so far. He had gotten us lost—and caused me to get cussed out. He had set off a land mine, left his grenades at an ambush site, and now fragged a 1,200-pound water buffalo. This was crazy! It was miraculous that he hadn't gotten us killed.

I was still calling out each man's name every night the way I'd promised, with the hope that Jesus would protect us. The Bible said that God loves every one of us, but I wondered about Bozo.

Did God love him too? Hmm... Yes, I'm sure He did, but I couldn't say the same.

I had a hard time with this guy. One thing was for sure though—Bozo was a man of action!

After all the excitement died down, we headed for the mountains, walking for a long time and covering quite a distance before we were ordered to move to a firebase in the "boonies." We climbed up hill after hill, humping for some time, before we reached the top.

We had been on this firebase before and I assumed we would do the same as we had always done. Usually we walked off the top of the hill and patrolled through the outlying area during the day, looking for signs of Charlie. Then maybe a squad of guys would go on an ambush at night, while the rest of us guarded the firebase perimeter.

This time it was different. The first couple of days we didn't have to patrol the area or go on ambush. We just guarded the perimeter at night and took it easy during the day. The supply chopper came in and landed, bringing mail and boxes from home. Getting mail did wonders for our spirits; if a box came from home with goodies, it was like Christmas or a birthday every time.

I had written home and complained about how bad I stunk because of the jungle rot. A couple of weeks later, the supply chopper brought me a box from my sweetheart. Thinking that it would be homemade chocolate chip cookies or brownies, I tore open the package—only to find plenty of Aqua Velva after-shave, deodorant, and some mouthwash. It was obvious that I had made a big mistake.

There was no way she could know that if I put that stuff on, Charlie would be able to sniff us out from miles away. The only value those things had here was their alcohol content. But, as I've said before, I wasn't a drinking hand and none of the guys were desperate enough to drink anything like that—yet. I should have written back home, telling her of my mistake and letting her know how wonderful cookies would make me smell, but I wasn't smart enough to handle things that smoothly.

Oh, well!

The next day, our platoon was called together and ordered to line up in platoon formation. That created chaos, with all of us laughing at Lt. Dennis and his order. We treated him like he was losing his mind. We hadn't been in a formation for months and it seemed ridiculous now. Formalities had become almost nonexistent among us. Why should today be any different?

Then the lieutenant spoke up and informed us that we were about to be served all the ice cream we could eat. If we wanted that to happen, we had better form up. It was hard to believe that ice cream was here, way back in the jungle-covered mountains of Vietnam. We moved right together into a nice tight formation in no time. He spoke up again and informed us that someone had been writing to his U.S. congressman, complaining about how poorly we were being treated. Today the Army was going to fix that by serving us ice cream.

"Would whoever was writing home complaining, please stop doing so?"

The Army wanted the lieutenant to pass that word to us.

Right!

Then we were marched a short distance to a serving area and dished up all the ice cream we could eat. That was the first and last time we were served ice cream in the field.

27

STANDING IN THE SHADOWS

It was early in the morning and the whole company was being airlifted by Hueys into a VC stronghold. In groups of six or seven, the grunts from Second Platoon, wearing helmets and loaded down with rucksacks, rifles, extra ammo, grenades, LAW rockets, mines, machine guns, canteens, food, and radios, were being loaded onto choppers. We clambered aboard and sat where we could. I ended up on the pilot's side of the chopper next to the rear door. We took off and rode for a half hour or so before beginning our descent. As we approached our landing site, we flew along a couple hundred feet above the ground.

Chick! Chick! Chick! Chick! Chick! Chick!

I heard a peculiar sporadic sound. It was quite unusual and could be heard even above the popping of the large overhead rotor blades. I looked all around the chopper to see if I could determine what was causing it, but couldn't find anything. Finally, I looked toward the window of the door beside me. There I discovered what the "chick, chick" sound was.

At eye level was a full-page Playboy centerfold in all her naked, voluptuous glory—with two bullet holes right through the paper where her belly button had been. Those bullets barely missed my head and I didn't even know it.

That sure took the fun out of the chopper ride. We were being hit by a lot of ground fire as we flew in low to land. The choppers set down in a clearing surrounded by trees, hedgerows, and rice paddies. Surprisingly, we didn't take any fire as we jumped to the ground. The Hueys lifted and were gone in no time. It didn't feel very good to just get dropped off and left in an unfamiliar war zone, especially after taking so many hits in the air!

We moved out right away through the trees and hedgerows, following a small path that headed toward a large river. We moved in single file and were spread out pretty well, with eight to ten feet between us. Gary, the preacher's kid who led Third Squad, was at the front of the patrol with me, behind our point man.

About 400 yards down the path we came across a Vietnamese man who looked to be about 30 years old. He was wearing dirty white shorts and a white shirt; not the usual dress. This looked very suspicious, so we stopped him for questioning. While making hair-cutting motions with his hands, he attempted broken English to let us know he was a barber. We were having a hard time getting any other information out of him.

Things weren't adding up. We knew that the area was full of VC, and this guy was of fighting age and wasn't dressed like a villager. We decided to take him with us and he reluctantly came along. We weren't going to leave any loose ends.

I could hear gunfire in the area near the river, but it wasn't coming our way. We kept moving down the narrow, winding path, knowing that we could set off booby traps at any time. All these operations were dangerous and scary. We had been in-country several months by that point, and I had somewhat adjusted to the constant danger. But I knew I could be gripped by fear out of nowhere, so I wasn't feeling cocky.

Gary and I were following the man on point. When we walked into an open area, we came upon another Vietnamese man that looked to be about 40 years old. He was very close to us, only about 13 feet away. We had surprised him. His dark hair was messed up and he wore a green shirt and pants that looked like a uniform. He held two Chicom hand grenades, one in each hand, and was walking sideways in front of us. He must have heard our choppers land and was trying to escape.

When I saw him, I threw my rifle up to my shoulder and

aimed at his heart, but I just didn't have it in me to outright shoot him dead. I could see the look of surprise and fear on his face when he saw three of us standing together, holding our rifles at a ready position. He twisted his hip toward me and I instantly lowered my sight and fired there. He spun around in a full circle.

I hadn't realized that Gary had fired at the same time I had. He bumped me on the shoulder.

"I hit him," he said.

At that point, I wasn't sure who had hit him, but it was plain to see that neither one of us had fired a deadly shot. I figured Gary to be a bad shot, but maybe not. I knew why I hadn't shot to kill. Right then I didn't have it in me to kill someone that close, while he looked straight at me. I wasn't that hard yet.

The wounded VC held onto his grenades and just sidled away from us toward the other soldiers. Papa shot and killed him.

We kept moving along, and as the path turned, we came upon an L-shaped bunker running along-side it, partially hidden among some trees. It was about eight feet long, and like most Vietnamese bunkers, had dirt mounded up about 30 inches above the ground. We could see a low opening at the long end and another at the short end facing the path.

About ten feet past it, on the other side of the path, rice was cooking on a small stove. I moved over to the long end of the bunker, pulled the pin on one of my grenades, and tossed it in the opening. Another soldier threw his grenade in the other opening. We stepped back.

BOOM! BOOM!

I thought if anyone was inside he would be dead for sure. I stepped on top of the mound and walked over to the opening at the short end.

Jerry and some more of our guys showed up with the barber, and they stood next to the cooking area. I could smell the rice still cooking on the small stove. I motioned for the barber to go into the bunker opening under me and bring out any bodies he found in there.

The opening was so low to the ground, he had to get down on his hands and knees to crawl inside. Jerry moved over behind the bunker, past the other opening. He stood there covering the area with his M16.

I could hear the gunfire that we had heard from across the river getting closer. A round or two snapped past us. I could also hear a machine gun firing in the distance. Other platoons were out there working the area, just like we were.

The barber crawled into the dark opening while I stood over the entrance watching him.

Cling-Pop!

I heard the metallic sound of a hand grenade being released, but it didn't register with me right then. I watched the barber hurriedly back his way out of the bunker and onto the path. He pointed toward the opening and started jabbering something I couldn't understand. I still stood on the bunker looking down at the opening.

BOOM!

Since the top of the bunker was about a foot-and-a-half thick, the dirt between the blast and me blocked most of the steel shrapnel, but the concussion knocked me silly. I could hardly stay on my feet and was in a daze for a few seconds. I glanced down at the entrance again and saw an arm sticking out, holding an American grenade.

How had this guy survived the blast from three grenades?

The arm snapped up, throwing the grenade just over my head. In my stupefied state, I saw it land between Jerry and me. My brain was telling me I was running, but my body wasn't moving. I knew we only had eight seconds to get away from the grenade once it was released. Precious time was ticking by. I saw Jerry dive for the ground.

The other men were near us as well, but all I could see was Jerry and the hand grenade. I'm sure everyone was scrambling to get away, but I was too stunned from the concussion to notice. I dropped to the ground and held onto my helmet. I could hear a lot of gunfire going on right behind me, but didn't know why.

When I hit the ground there were only about three seconds left until the grenade would blow. I started counting. I wasn't afraid. It was all happening too quickly. I counted from one to twelve and nothing happened.

I slowly raised my helmet with one hand, and could see the grenade lying four feet from me. Jerry was four feet on the other side of it, raising his helmet at the same time. We just looked at each other. His face had an astonished look like nothing I had seen before. We stood up together.

I got the feeling we were standing on holy ground and, by the look on Jerry's face, we were. We carefully moved away, trying to tiptoe, knowing that somehow our lives had been spared. We never talked about it. It was too improbable to discuss.

There is an old song that we sang in church when I was a kid that went like this:

"Standing somewhere in the shadows you'll find Jesus. He's the Friend who always cares and understands. Standing somewhere in the shadows you will find Him…"[12]

I didn't see Him in the shadows, but I believed He was close by somewhere.

I believed that we had help staying alive that day and I was very thankful. We'd been in a very dangerous situation, and I didn't take it lightly that we had been spared.

We still needed to set up a perimeter for the night, so we moved out. My ears were ringing like crazy, but my head was still on my shoulders and I was thankful for that. I didn't want to think about what would have happened to Jerry and me if…

28

DIRTY WORDS

The military has one word it can't exist without. That four-letter word is used to describe everything, and is commonly used multiple times in most sentences. In various forms it is used as a noun, a verb, an adverb, an adjective, and every other part of speech. My father would not tolerate us using it, or others like it, at any time.

Growing up we had very few restrictions set by our father, but it was well understood that there were five major rules, and if violated, would cost us plenty:

1. Don't bring the cops home.
2. Don't drink liquor.
3. Don't act disrespectfully toward women.
4. Don't swear.
5. Do what Dad tells you to do.

Those were the standards he'd set and lived.

I had violated most of these rules at one point or another, and it had always cost me something.

Dad had done his part to keep us on track. Aside from those rules, we'd been given plenty of freedom. He expected us to know what was right by watching him and thinking for ourselves.

Dad's gas station was in a small town in the Central Valley of California. The seasonal farm hands worked through the summer, and saved what little money they could to see them through the winter months.

When there wasn't enough work for them to make ends meet all the way 'til spring, they would come to Dad's station.

Gas was about 30¢ a gallon then, and Dad loaned them money for groceries and gave them gas on credit.

Each family had a little credit book with their name on it. Each time Dad helped them, they signed for it with either their name, or an "X" if they couldn't write. His desk was full of these little books and he didn't charge any interest on the loans. When spring came and they found work, they'd start paying him back. This went on for years.

The railroad tracks were about a half-block from the gas station. In those days, most of the homeless had been hobos, winos, or bums. Dad got to know most of them by name. Very often, one of these guys would get off the train and come see Dad for a handout. Some of them he paid to do small jobs around the station. Some he took to the grocery store and bought staples such as bread, canned soup, and lunchmeat before they went on their way. Others he took to the cafe next door and bought lunch. I went along a couple of times when he did that.

The first thing Dad wanted when he got home from work was a hug and a kiss from Mom. It was easy to tell how much he loved her. He set a good example for me. He took our family to church regularly, where sometimes people stood up and talked about how God had helped them. Most of the time I found it pretty boring, but if Dad stood up to speak, I always sat up and listened. I knew that he would only talk in front of people if he had something of real value to say.

He almost never disciplined us. Mom had taken care of that. Her discipline happened often and we'd gotten used to it. She didn't have what it took to put the fear of God into us. She was merciful and simply didn't have the strength.

Once in seventh grade, my hunting/fishing buddy Kenny and I had been cutting up in history class while the teacher was talking. When the teacher finally had enough, he gave us a choice: four hours of homework or a swat in front of the class.

Heck, I can take whatever he can dish out.

I chose the swat.

So did Kenny.

We moved to the front of the class. Kenny wanted to go first. He had no idea what was coming, and neither did I.

"Bend over and take hold of the desk," the teacher instructed Kenny.

With paddle in hand, the young, and we soon found out, strong, teacher stood behind him. Kenny never looked back, but when that paddle lifted him six inches off the floor with a loud pow, he'd let out a whistle like a kettle blowing off a full head of steam.

I tried not to laugh.

Kenny limped back to his seat and could hardly sit down.

Whoa! My turn.

I got exactly what I'd asked for—the same treatment.

Class continued with everyone listening up really well for a long time. They were afraid of getting what we'd gotten.

After a while the teacher cleared his throat.

"Kenny, Bob, you took your punishment well," he said. "I have to respect you for that."

It had been nice of him to say, and we never needed another "up-lifting." We considered these kinds of experiences like badges of courage but hadn't gone looking for them.

That kind of thing usually didn't get home to our parents, but one day my older brother Don got into a fight at school.

"You S-O-B," he yelled at the other guy.

The teacher called home and Dad got the message. We all knew what that meant. Don wasn't in trouble for the fight, he could have had good reason for that; but as far as Dad was concerned, there was never a good reason for swearing. It was near the end of the school year and the weather was hot. Dad usually got home late, around eight.

Don was a good brother. He always shared with me and kept an eye out for me. I could count on him. He helped me learn how to believe in myself. My oldest brother Dewey and I were sitting with him under the swamp cooler in the hallway with the cool air blowing on us. We were trying to console him because we knew what was coming down when Dad got home.

Dad stepped through the front door.

"Don, to the back yard!" he said.

That had been as bad as life could get. All the powers that be would be unleashed, we thought.

Woeful cries came from the backyard, but it was over quickly. My dad always handled discipline with restraint. He loved us all and had done his part to keep us within boundaries, which was no small chore.

Dad was big on us earning our own money. When I was old enough, I started working in the potato sheds unloading trucks. In the summer we worked long hours to make spending money. I started picking up some bad language on the job and had gotten pretty proficient at it. I had been working so many long, hard hours that I started talking in my sleep but didn't know it.

Early one morning while I was getting ready for work, Mom came in to my bedroom.

"Bob, I heard the strangest thing late last night," she said. "It sounded like there was a foul-talking sailor in your room. You haven't picked up some bad words at work, have you?"

"Oh no, Mom," I said, "I must have been dreaming—and you never know what you're saying when you're dreaming."

Mom was giving me a heads-up and I took it. My father didn't liked filthy speech and wanted us to come up with better ways of expressing ourselves. He'd lived it himself and believed we could too.

After a short leave at home, when I was heading for Hawaii—and ultimately Vietnam—Dad and Mom stood on the front porch together, watching as Beth and I left for the airport. We had said our good-byes, and I looked back as we got in the car and saw my father's head down, with tears on his face.

"I wonder why he's crying," I said to Beth as we drove away.

I guess he knew far more about war than I did.

My father had taught me some valuable things, and because of him, it had never been okay with me to swear.

I found myself having to really work on coming up with creative expressions in the Army, but it was worth it.

29

THE GREAT OUTDOORS

We headed for the mountains with our rucksacks stuffed full, all we could carry on our backs, and more hanging off our pistol belts. I mentioned earlier that there was always plenty I didn't know when we headed out, and it was no different this time. I didn't know what the mission was, and I didn't know when we would be coming back. However, I did know that we were headed west into the mountainous jungle, and I knew that I had just over 200 days to go before my "Army Studies" course was over.

I was no short-timer and neither were my buddies; most of us had arrived here at the same time. As time went on, some men in our platoon were traded to other units and new guys were brought in to take their places. That way, when it was time for us to go home (fingers crossed), our whole platoon wouldn't leave the company all at once.

Some new guys had joined us earlier. The afternoon "TC" had gotten off the chopper, he was sent to my position. He didn't appear nervous, but when I'd asked him to dig us a foxhole for the night, he didn't hesitate. I was pleasantly surprised to see he had finished a three-foot regulation foxhole in short order. The only thing missing was the grenade hole at the bottom. When I pointed that out, he took care of it right away. Cool! I hadn't had a foxhole that nice in all the time I had been in-country. This guy was going to work out just fine.

That night I pulled the first hour guard; then it was his turn. It had to have been real scary for him on his first night in the field, staring into total darkness and listening to unfamiliar noises. He got settled in the foxhole and I hit the sack. After about 15 minutes, I got up to see how he was doing. I checked his M16. He had it on full auto. I didn't want him to shoot me by accident—I was capable of doing that myself. I had him flip it to safety and assured him he could get it off quickly, if need be. I hadn't forgotten how frightened I was my first months out in the field.

TC got his nickname because he sounded like the cartoon character Top Cat. He settled in to soldiering and soon became a friend. Shortly after his arrival, I noticed every now and then that my chow was missing from my rucksack in the mornings. Since TC was a real chow-hound, I think he might have helped himself as payback for digging me that fancy foxhole his first night.

Loaded down, we climbed into the mountains and walked through the jungle for days looking for Charlie. Like always, he was hard to find.

One day, on a small tree-covered hill, we set the machine gun down and the platoon took a much-needed rest. We were in a "free-fire zone" that was off limits to everyone, so we were surprised to see rice paddies, in good condition, in front of us. It was obvious someone had been caring for them.

While we were sitting there, we saw a gook coming from the side, about 300 yards below. As he crossed in front of us, we motioned for him to come up. Instead, he started running. That wasn't a smart move to make in front of target-hungry GIs.

Jerry was ready on the machine gun and was right on him. The guy was fast and I watched the bullets draw closer and closer behind him as he ran for all he was worth.

Jerry was closing the gap and bullets were hitting at his heels. In another second, the gook would be lying dead in the rice paddies. He must have realized this because he fell to his knees and raised both hands, jabbering for mercy.

Jerry promptly stopped shooting and we again motioned

for him to come up to us. This time he did, without hesitation. Jerry wasn't out to kill for no reason and showed restraint by letting him live.

The man was questioned, given some good advice about the danger he was in, and sent on his way. I wondered if he knew how close he had been to dying. He had one heck of a story to tell his mama-san that night about the wonderful GIs who let him go.

As we continued west, sometimes chopping our way through the foliage, going up and down hills and mountains, crossing little valleys and streams, we moved deeper and deeper into the desolate jungle. It was so beautiful. It looked like no human had ever been there. The country was filled with colors, sights, smells, and sounds that I had never experienced.

Once, when I'd had my nose in the grass trying to hide from a sniper, I saw movement in front of my eyes. I focused on what I thought was a four-inch worm. No! It was a snake, wiggling along with its little forked-tongue and diamond-shaped head about eight inches from my face. I sure was glad he wasn't big! The sniper was enough to deal with.

Another time, we were humping through triple-canopy jungle and we crossed paths with a troop of some kind of monkeys swinging through the treetops. They were there one second—and gone the next.

After we trudged up a long, steep ridge, we stopped to catch our breath. Spreading out, we sat along the path to take a quick break. Everyone, that is, except Frank. He didn't sit down. He was carrying the 23-pound machine gun and his overloaded rucksack full of all the regular stuff, as well as: thick, hardback books; old, extra C-rations; chunks of chewing tobacco; cans of snuff; and a 25-pound brass Buddha he had swiped from who-knows-where.

It was very muggy and we were all soaked with sweat, but Frank acted like this was a Sunday afternoon walk in the park. He stood there with his long arms held up to the sky, nodding his head in amazement as he looked out over the valley below.

"Holy cow, can you believe how gorgeous this country is?" he proclaimed. "Only God Himself could make something this beautiful!"

Did he have heat stroke?

No, the truth of the matter was that Frank had a great appreciation for nature, even when it was filled with danger.

We had been busting our rears for weeks without any contact and were now linking up with the rest of our company at a very wide river. Word was that Laos was just on the other side, if we could manage to get across. It had rained recently and the water was high and deceptively smooth. In an effort to cross, one of the guys from First Platoon waded out holding one end of a rope while several men held on to the other end. As he ventured into the current, he was swept away, carried down-river through the jungle, disappearing in an instant. We felt helpless. None of us were ready for that to happen. He was gone so fast there was nothing we could do to retrieve him. Days later, his body was recovered by the ARVNs.

We patrolled the area for days without making any real contact with the enemy. It seemed like a long, hard nature walk, leeches and all, but we had to be prepared for much more than that.

Most of the time it seemed like Charlie wasn't anywhere around, even though we were on his turf. He patiently waited for us to get in a position where he would be in control. He constantly watched to see if we were lax in our ways or if there was anything he could use in his favor. Did we keep our guard up? Did we do foolish things, like travel the same path often or at the same time of day? Did we stay in one spot too long?

It was tiring to have to go the long way around, chopping our way through elephant grass or the bush, when it looked so much easier to take a short cut. But we knew he was waiting for an ideal opportunity.

Because we hadn't made contact, we became lax and one afternoon had not set up a good perimeter. A Huey pilot actually managed to back his chopper down through an opening in the triple-canopy jungle and set it down. He made an amazing landing, bringing in much-needed supplies.

But while the chopper sat there with its big rotor turning and men hurrying to unload, gunfire erupted! I was standing behind the tail rotor and looked up toward the front of the Huey. I saw four gooks standing on a small berm to one side of the chopper, firing their automatic weapons into the front of it. Their weapons emptied in seconds. They ran back into the thick jungle and were gone. The pilot had to get back out of that tight spot, so he powered up the chopper and turned at the same time. The chopper was shaking like crazy but was able to climb out through the treetops.

All of this happened in an unbelievable blur. The Huey had to have taken over a hundred rounds. I never found out what damage or injuries were caused.

Another time, we set up our perimeter early one night, deep in the jungle at the end of a long, narrow valley. Just as it was getting dark, one of the new guys started flicking a cigarette lighter near me. I advised him that he might not want to keep that up.

"Hey Knucklehead, you make a great target," I admonished him.

"There's no one out there, Whitworth," he argued. "What's stuck up your rear? This little lighter isn't going to hurt anything."

It was true, we hadn't seen signs of anyone.

Two more little flicks and a bullet whizzed between us and hit the dirt. It was obvious that the bullet had been fired from a long way off. Whoever fired that shot was no hick VC; he knew something about bullet trajectory.

Charlie just couldn't pass up the opportunity that this foolish action had provided. I was relieved to be hidden by darkness, and flicker-boy had learned a good lesson.

It was close calls like this that kept me praying for all of us, even though I had doubts at times. I still said each man's name to Him every night, with hope that He would continue to keep us all alive.

James, in the New Testament, said that the prayer of a righteous man is powerful and effective.[13] I didn't view myself as righteous, but I did keep praying. It's not like I could presume that we would stay alive by my request—we were in a war zone, after all.

Even though I knew there were others praying for our safety besides me, what if I didn't get the answer I was looking for? What about all those who had prayed and been prayed for who lost their lives or were maimed? What would happen to my faith if one of these guys got killed?

What I wanted were answers that simply weren't available to me. I was in a trial like nothing I ever dreamed possible. But, regardless of the lack of apparent answers to my questions, I had faith that my prayers were being heard.

I lived with the guys in my platoon day in and day out. They were tough men and had the kind of grit I admired. I was nobody special, but it was clear to them that I knew what I believed. They knew I didn't drink or swear, and if I slipped and said "Shit," my close buddies would call me on it.

"What'd you say?"

They could spot a phony a mile away and showed no respect for one, so I would straighten up and take their admonition.

When we pulled bunker guard at the LZs we usually had time to kill, so we'd talk about everything. Girls were always a good topic, as were cars. The stories could go on forever. Then there was food. At times we made ourselves so hungry we could almost smell the home cooking.

Because of the situation we were in, and knowing death

could be near for any one of us, sometimes we talked about God. Death was like the elephant in the room. We knew it was there but we didn't want to talk about it very much. It was a part of what war was about and most of the time was very frightening to face. I didn't like thinking about it, but it always seemed so close.

Sometimes we talked about our beliefs. Most guys believed in prayer and I was sure when they were under heavy pressure they would pray. We would get to discussing this, and one of them might say he was good. He'd done some good things and some bad things in his life, and the good things stacked up higher than the bad things, so he figured God would let him into heaven when he died. That's what seemed fair to him: that everything would work out fine.

Then someone else would say that he'd done a few good things and a lot of bad things, and he would probably be going to hell, but he wasn't too worried about it. Maybe someday he would clean up his act so he could go somewhere nice when he died.

Somebody usually brought up the idea that life just started somehow and we slowly became humans, and that when we died, we were just dead, and it would be as if we never existed. Then there would be the guy who didn't seem to care at all about God. He just wanted to live through the war. He liked his vices: smoking, drinking, loose women, and doing a few drugs. If he got in a tight spot and needed a little help, he might pray, but he didn't want anyone or anything nailing down what was right or wrong and interfering with his fun.

The pressure I felt from the dangerous times we were experiencing caused me to look intently at my own beliefs. James also said in the Bible, to keep our faith and endure our trials because they can make us better.[14] That's what I had to do. I had to count on the fact that enduring through these times would produce something in me that was worthwhile. If what I had been taught and had hoped for could be washed out in a life-and-death situation, I needed to know.

It wasn't any fun.

Not only was it not fun, it was painful. I was packing around some agonizing grief that I didn't want to face, let alone deal with. I hoped to build a stronger position of faith in Jesus. What I understood about "hope" was like thinking of something you wanted with no idea whether you could actually get it. That seemed like a weak concept. When fatigue set in, hope could slip away. It didn't seem like much to stake my soul on, but I was doing it anyway, even though I hadn't yet grasped the connection between hope and trust.[15]

30

RED-HEADED SNAKE

We were working around the mountains out of LZ Ryder, about 25 miles from the Laotian border. We wore ourselves out looking for Charlie and his supplies, with little to show for our labors. At least we hadn't been ambushed, and there seemed to be fewer mines in the jungle. Late one morning we found a narrow path going up a ridge, with high brush and trees on both sides, and followed it for a while. Word was passed back to stop and set up an ambush right on the path.

Right!

There was no room to do that. The lieutenant had just decided to take a long break here, and we were ready for it. We had good cover and would be able to spread out in the green brush to relax for a while.

We were taking it easy and some of the guys, including Jerry, were getting some much needed sleep. Jerry had been packing the machine gun and was glad for the chance to set it down in front of him while he rested against a small tree. Sleep was hard to come by, so whenever we had a chance to get some in a relatively safe place, we took advantage of the opportunity.

I liked Jerry. He was fair-minded and handled his duties responsibly. He always took his turn carrying the 23-pound machine gun. He wasn't a big guy, but that didn't matter. He would still lift the heavy gun up and sling it over his shoulder, with the 100-round belt of 7.62 ammo folded back over the breach cover, and chug along all day. When Jerry and I had that encounter with the grenade awhile back, it connected us somehow.

As I sat across from the snoozing Jerry, I looked down the path and saw movement in the low brush. A six-foot long snake, about an inch-and-a-half in diameter, came out onto the path. It was solid red from the tip of its nose to eight inches back on its body where it then turned a solid shiny green all the way to the end of its tail. It moved along swiftly and didn't show any sign of being afraid of us. Then, behind it, I saw another, identical snake.

Yikes! Were these snakes dangerous?

They sure looked like it. They raced in and out between us like they were playing. Guys started throwing helmets at them, as well as whatever else they could get their hands on. The snakes seemed to enjoy it, like it was a game. They were fast and moved quickly out of the way of the flying objects.

We didn't want to shoot because it would give our position away. I stood up, pulled my .45 pistol from its holster and threw it at one of them—and missed, the same as everyone else. The snake swerved as it went right on by. I could hear commotion from the other guys as the snakes moved up the path. At least they were away from me!

I picked up my pistol, looked it over, shoved it back in the holster, and sat back down across from Jerry. When the snakes came back ten minutes later, he was still enjoying his sleep. They seemed to be having fun as they raced past us down the path. One of them stopped, turned back, and headed toward us. I watched as the snake slithered up and coiled between Jerry's legs. It raised its head, swayed back and forth, its long red tongue flicking in and out, and looked right at Jerry's peacefully sleeping face.

This was too good to be true! The snake was in the middle of the path, ignoring me, with its head about two feet from Jerry's. I felt it was my duty to warn him. This was great! I couldn't believe my good fortune—an opportunity to be a genuine hero. I waited a few seconds.

"Hey, Jerry," I said quietly, as I touched his boot with mine.

He opened his eyes and I thought he was going to give birth. Then he exploded—his helmet flying off as he hit it with his arm trying to get up and away. His leg jerked straight out, knocking the machine gun over with his boot. His eyes almost bugged out of his head. He was a flashing blur of moving body parts and dirty, green, smelly fatigues as he babbled some fearful plea for help. Maybe he thought he was in some kind of nightmare; I'm sure he hadn't known there were snakes around.

I couldn't stop laughing; I thought I was going to die because my belly hurt so much. Jerry was standing a bit away from me on the edge of the path, breathing deeply, and trying to get hold of himself. He didn't think it was so funny. How was I to know Jerry would be so terrified of a little red-headed snake? The snake had disappeared. I didn't know where it went, but I was sure glad it had come by to visit.

I was tired after all the excitement and could have used a nap, but I was a little worried about falling asleep with Jerry watching out for me.

We had been in the jungle for a long time and finally began working our way back to the flats. We still had a way to go before we would be out. We hadn't gotten mail and packages from home for quite a while because the choppers couldn't get down through the triple canopy. We also hadn't been able to wash or do anything to care for our bodies, and the rain falling on us every afternoon only made it worse. Most of us had rotting feet. We were walking gardens of fungus. It was on our arms and other unmentionable places. Since the weather was always humid, and we were humping through jungle, we stayed soaked with sweat. Maybe Charlie could smell us and didn't really need to see us to know where we were.

Finally, the area opened up a little. Late in the day we reached a place next to a hill where a chopper could make it in. A Huey landed and unloaded letters and boxes from home, as well as some chow. Then it left us, like it always did. It would have been great to have had an excuse to catch a ride back.

The good thing, though, was that I now had 14 boxes from home. The bad thing was, that I also had 14 boxes to hump up a hill and get set up for the night.

I was carrying the M60 that day, which didn't help. There was no way I could carry all those boxes up that hill by myself, and the guys were already leaving. Most of them had boxes too, and couldn't wait to get to the top, make camp, and rip open those goodie-filled packages. It was a long climb up and Jerry didn't seem to want to help me after the fun-filled snake experience.

I offered to share with anyone who would help pack stuff up the hill, but they were all on the move except Lewis, standing behind me, who was packing the radio. It weighed over 25 pounds and he had a box or two of his own to carry.

"Hey Bob, I'll help. Give me some of those boxes."

"Darn, Lewis," I said, "you're too good to me. Thanks a million."

He walked over and started stacking boxes in and on my pack. I put five boxes on his pack and he carried a couple in his arms. I stacked a couple more on the machine gun I had slung in front of me.

Lewis had a quiet strength that could always be counted on. I didn't know if he just couldn't stand to see the goodies left where Charlie would find them later, or what, but I sure was thankful for his help. We were both going to break a sweat getting those boxes to the top of that hill. Off we went, plodding up to the top. Everything would be just fine as long as we didn't step on a mine and blow chocolate chip cookies all over the hillside.

When we finally made it to the top and had our perimeter set up, we chowed down. We just sort of piled the goodies in one place and pigged out. It was so great! Some of the things we got from home we would never have eaten stateside. One was called Shake-a-Puddin'. The reason we loved it was that it was lightweight, there were several in a pack, and all we had to do was add water, shake, and voila! Pudding! This was kid's stuff, but out here it was the closest thing to ice cream we could get.

The higher-ups had let up on us pulling ambushes every night for a while. We had become so tired that we would go out and hide, with one or two guys on watch, while the rest of us slept. I don't know if they knew this or not, and didn't care, but shortly after we started doing that it seemed like they let up on us. We still pulled ambushes, but not as often.

In the morning, we headed down the hill toward the rice paddies. Around noon we were well into them and got word there was enemy activity at the village in front of us. There were going to be air strikes coming in soon. It was wide-open paddies between the village and us so we moved to within 1,000 yards and waited.

The village was hit with napalm and 250-pound bombs. After the jets made several runs, they lifted and we moved into the burned-out area, which was now nothing but ashes with big holes blown in the ground. The trees were burnt and small bunkers had been exposed, but there weren't any people. It was black, hot, and smoky.

The area was small, and didn't take long to go through. On the way out, we walked past the body of a young woman who had been sexually assaulted and killed. Her exposed body lay on the ash-covered ground with the cruel implement still protruding. It was an unpleasant sight. We had no idea how or why this had happened. Certainly some very cruel things had taken place here. She lay on top of the ashes as though someone had put her there after the explosions so we would be sure to see her.

We had been humping the mountains and jungle for six or seven weeks, living out of our rucksacks. We weren't kids anymore. We had some real hard lessons under our belts now.

And there were more to come.

31

GRENADES

The choppers dropped us off at LZ Amy, deep in the mountains of Quang Nai province, to be perimeter guards, and to get some rest. We were assigned positions, so we put our ponchos together to make little shelters to sleep under and protect us from the rain.

We had gotten used to a meager lifestyle and expected nothing more. Hot meals were delivered as long as the weather didn't keep the choppers from coming in. After being there a few days, medics were flown in to give us a bunch of inoculations. They didn't say what for, but soon each of us had many new holes.

While guarding this LZ, we had four men assigned to each position. That meant each man had to pull two hours of watch, which was easy. Much of the time we would have three men in each position, and once in a while only two men. The fewer men per position, the more watch hours you had to pull, so having four men was really great. Heck, with only two hours to pull, you wouldn't have to slap yourself to stay awake.

Alone in our positions, sometimes scared, sometimes bored, we were always sleepy. Falling asleep was dangerous for everyone. If your buddies caught you sleeping, they had a right to be mad and could give you an unpleasant awakening. If the sarge caught you, you would be up on charges. If Charlie caught you, you'd be dead.

After pulling guard, I'd wake up the next guy for his turn. It was important to familiarize myself with my buddies' peculiarities. For instance, Ace could carry on a conversation with you—in his sleep. His voice varied slightly in tone when awake and asleep. When it was time to wake him for his turn, I had to talk to him for a while, listening carefully, until I heard his voice change. Then I knew he was awake. Otherwise, I might check on him a few minutes later to find that he had walked from his position back to where he had been sleeping, having never been awake at all.

Then there were times when things were just plain peculiar. When we first got in-country, a fellow pulled bunker guard one night with a fifth of whiskey and a case of grenades. We were in the mountains on a hilltop. I was a few bunkers down and could see that when he first started drinking, he threw the grenades way out in front of him. As it got dark I could see the explosions even better. An hour or so later, the exploding grenades were so close to him in midair that I'd thought for sure he would soon be injured.

But, he kept drinking and throwing grenades. I was positive he would be dead before morning. My watch ended and I hit the sack. He must have run out of grenades before he could blow himself off the top of the bunker because I saw him, hung-over, the next day.

Most of the time we didn't have any extra explosives to mess with in the field. If you had to pack it, you only carried what you needed. But that didn't mean we wouldn't try. Once I discovered that a radar installation we were guarding had a large supply of munitions, including cases of quarter-pound TNT blocks.

I told Frank about it. I'd never played with TNT blocks before and wondered if a grenade fuse would screw into a TNT block. I tried it and it worked. There was really no good reason to do this, but it sounded different when it went off. I figured if I fixed several blocks together, I could get a really big bang. But that never happened. I realized I wouldn't be able to throw it far enough to keep it from blowing me away.

Frank and I once got ourselves a case of grenades when we pulled guard at night, and lobbed them down the hill to keep ourselves entertained. His position was a little way from mine and I could hear his grenades go off. If Charlie wanted to probe the perimeter and saw this stuff going off in front of us, he would pick somewhere else to try it.

After about a week, we got bored of simply throwing them over the side of the hill. I thought it would be fun for us to start playing a little game of "chicken." After we pulled the pin, we let the handle fly and counted to see how long we could hold on before throwing it away. We had eight seconds once we let the handle go until it exploded. When it rained, we needed to be a little more careful. If your foot slipped in the mud while counting, the game would be over. We were having lots of fun with our quick-count grenade game.

Frank showed up at my guard position one night in the rain. His eyes were as big as his snuff tins. He insisted he wasn't playing this game anymore. He explained how he had pulled the pin, let the handle fly, and started counting. He got to four and froze. He said it exploded right in front him, in midair, just after he came to his senses and threw it. He swore he didn't know how he had lived through the explosion. He was acting as if he had just lived through a near-death experience or something. I wanted to jokingly remind him of the near-death experience he had given me on our first ambush together, but he was too serious. I would have to wait before I started calling him a sissy. We gave up on the quick-count game for then.

When Boredom shows up, he always brings his friends: Ignorance, Stupidity, and Over-Confidence. They showed up every now and then and didn't care who they hung out with. They spent time with the officers and us lowly grunts alike. I had a hard time getting rid of them.

They showed up one night when I came up with the idea to mess around with trip-flares. I removed the handle by holding it and pulling the pin. Then I slid the pin back under the handle over the spring cap. Even though it would be quieter if it were tripped on an ambush, the whole idea didn't make good sense. Somehow that didn't matter because I tried it more than once. The last time, however, I slipped and the flare went off while I was trying to put the trip-pin back over the cap as I held it close to my face.

Pow!

When it went off, it burned my upper lip, taking off half my mustache and singeing my eyebrows. Now I really felt smart! I knew I couldn't count on any sympathy from the guys. They didn't suffer fools well, and besides, they were looking for a good laugh as much as I was. I wasn't going to get let off the hook.

Dang!

Maybe I was suffering from too many concussions.

32

LUCKY SHOT

A day or so later I was walking behind the ordnance bunker just as Lt. Dennis came out with a case of M72 LAW rockets. I liked this five-pound fiberglass rocket. The tube was about 25 inches long, three inches in diameter, and the rocket could penetrate 12 inches of solid steel.

To fire one, you pulled a couple of pins, telescoped it out to 35 inches, and it was ready to go. Laying it on your shoulder, you looked through a pop-up peep sight, and squeezed a rubber button. It fired, with the blast going out the back of the tube as the rocket launched. It was accurate and went a long way, but was only good for one shot. After you fired it, you slammed the empty fiberglass tube against a tree or something, breaking it into useless pieces to throw away.

"Let's shoot some of these things!" he said.

Cool!

We walked to the edge of the perimeter and looked down at some trees about 500 yards away, picking one as a target. The lieutenant fired a couple of rockets but didn't hit the tree. He picked up another LAW, pulled the pins, stretched it out, and handed it to me. I laid it on my shoulder, looked down the tube, put the crosshairs on the trunk, and squeezed the button.

BOOM!

The rocket flew toward the tree, hitting it in the center. It fell to the ground with a crash.

Holy cow! Lucky shot!

We fired a couple more rockets, just goofing off.

I liked Lt. Dennis; he was younger than most of us but had a good head on his shoulders and wasn't too full of himself. He knew there were plenty of problems we had to deal with and he stuck up for us.

As a kid I'd hunted jackrabbits—too much of the time, according to Dad. The farmers wanted the rabbits gone and I enjoyed the target practice. I invited a new kid in town to go hunting with me. We both took our .22 rifles and were hunting in a large open field with some short brush. When a jackrabbit jumped up in front of us about 40 yards out, and another four rabbits started running along behind the first one, he just stood there. The rabbits were all in a big hurry and I had quickly thrown up my rifle, shot the last rabbit first, and then shot the four in front of him.

Wow! I never shot that many jackrabbits at one time.

I lowered my rifle and looked at him wondering why he hadn't shot. I thought he was going to tell me what a good shot I'd been.

"You don't give anybody else a chance to shoot!" he blurted.

Heck, shooting rabbits was no waiting game. It was obvious he had never hunted them before. If I'd have been with my regular hunting buddies, I might not have even gotten off a shot!

Hunting and shooting at Charlie was certainly nothing like hunting jackrabbits. The only thing that was similar was, that when we did make contact with Charlie, he often would be running away like a scared rabbit.

Charlie was hard to find and it seemed like he shot at us more than we did at him. He had the advantage of shooting at us from well-hidden spots: in thick bushes, behind trees, and from holes he could quickly duck back into. Most of the time bullets started cracking between us seemingly out of nowhere.

When we did see him, the military wanted us to shout three times, "Dung lai! Dung lai! Dung lai!" ("Stop!") before opening fire. Sometimes we would say it, but that only gave him a head start on our bullets if he even heard us. He was hard to hit because he would zigzag left and right. We would just get flashes of him running through trees or a village. He was usually a long way off and breaking a speed record. Running fast wasn't a problem when bullets were chasing you. Putting distance between us always helped him. None of that movie stuff where the good guy doesn't run out of bullets and never misses. If we got a good shot, it was because Charlie made a bad mistake, and that didn't happen very often.

While out in the mountains like this we didn't get as much sniper fire as in the flat country. We had been on this hill for a couple of weeks and we were sure to be leaving soon. The Brass never let us stay in one place very long.

We left the LZ and headed down out of the mountains. After a few days we could see the rice paddies stretching out in front of us. Between us and the flat country was a pass through the mountains we had used several times. It was the best way down, but now there was concern that Charlie might have noticed how much we traveled it and could be waiting to ambush us.

Steve, in Second Squad, was a farm boy from Kansas. His blonde curly hair gave him a boyish look that he would soon lose. He had the job of walking point and was more than a little worried. I thought he was likely to run into trouble too, so I gave him my little Bible with the metal plate to put in his shirt pocket. It couldn't hurt. We ended up worrying for nothing, and hours later stepped out into the rice paddies. We continued on and set up for the night in a graveyard. The graves provided mounds we could sleep beside.

Word came that First Platoon had drawn sniper fire while on patrol. As their lieutenant directed his men, a deadly bullet from the sniper hit him. His death sent the reality home to hit the ground immediately when shooting started, reminding us that Charlie didn't always miss.

We got started early the next morning. It was another wretched day. By late afternoon, at least we hadn't run into any trouble. I was clumping through a rice paddy with Gramps behind me, when sniper fire started in on us from one of the villages about 400 yards away. Everyone scattered out across the paddy trying to avoid getting hit. Gramps and I didn't move quickly enough.

Snap!

A round went right between us.

Splat!

Down we went into the mud! We lay as close to a dike as we could, trying to hide.

Dad-gum it!

I was hoping to make it back to LZ Bronco without feeling like a mud-ball.

Gramps was no happier about this than I was. We needed to stay down in this muck awhile and give Charlie time to get nervous about us calling in artillery on his position. After a bit, Gramps slowly stood up, dripping with stinky mud, and pointed out the water leeches sizing me up.

"Gramps," I said, "you can jaw on about anything you want as long as you're playing target to see if Charlie's gone."

Gramps was always carrying on about things going wrong and how he'd had to fix 'em.

Sure, Gramps, you're my hero.

We made it to the firebase and set up for the night. I wrote home to my folks and told them about the sniper. I didn't often write about what our days were really like, but I needed to tell them a little something every once in a while.

In the morning I heard some news about a friend of mine in another company. Robbie and I had both been drafted at the same time from the San Francisco Bay Area and had run into each other off and on ever since. Unfortunately, he had tripped a booby trap while crossing a bridge. It cost him an eye and killed one of the guys with him.

The last time I had seen Robbie was one morning on the

bunker line when he dropped by for a visit. He looked as if he had tried to make love to a tiger. His fatigues were all ripped to shreds and he had deep scratches everywhere. I asked him why he was in such a well-kept manner.

"Have you ever tried to make it through the triple-barbed wire protecting our perimeter?" he asked me.

"No." I answered.

"Well," he replied, "it's no problem after you down a fifth of Vietnamese Very Very Old Crow Whisky."

During our time at the base, I was informed that I had been promoted to "Spec. 4." That meant I would be making $195 a month plus $65 combat pay. There were still plenty of higher-ranking people who were telling me what to do, but it was nice to know I was at least up a notch. I was on this job 24/7, which meant I was earning roughly 36¢ an hour while minimum wage back home was $1.65. There were other benefits though…I had great outdoor accommodations, occasionally got a hot meal, and had all the C-rations I could carry.

33

CROSSFIRE

Our company was loaned out to another brigade and we were working in the fields along the coast outside LZ Baldy in the northeast corner of Quang Tin province. The rainy season had started and the monsoons were upon us. It rained constantly and the amount of water coming out of the sky was almost unbelievable. It had rained on us a lot since we arrived in-country, but now it was torrential. When we trained in Hawaii it had rained hard in the mountains, but we didn't have to stay out in it all the time.

Charlie had more sense than we did, so he was even harder to find when the weather was bad. We were always out there, soaked to the bone, looking for him. One evening, after setting up our perimeter, the usual artillery was called in around us while we put up our little makeshift poncho-covers.

The only thing that gave me comfort during this time was the tough air mattress we all carried with us. Being left outside so long in the driving rain like mangy dogs, I don't know how I could have stayed healthy without it. When the ground was covered with water, I would blow up the mattress and attempt to spend the night afloat. If I could keep the top part of my body on the mattress, it would stay dry, and I could sleep.

We continued working in the flats close to the beach. We were on search maneuvers with M113 armored personnel carriers that we called "APCs" or "tracks." These light-armored vehicles could carry eight grunts and a four-man crew, and gave us added protection while we were on patrol. The rain had let up and we had been hard at it all day. We came through a small village late in the day, searched it, and found nothing. I noticed that a little cane bed had been left in one of the hooches and I got the bright idea to borrow it for the night.

The APCs headed off somewhere else, so our platoon located a place to spend the night. The rain had stopped, which was good, because I wanted to sleep on this little bed. It was 15 or 16 inches off the ground, and just big enough to hold me. You think I would have learned by then that some of my ideas needed more critical thought.

We set up our perimeter in an open sandy area with trees sparsely scattered behind us. I carried the little bed out there and put it down where Frank and I were setting up for the night. We had a pretty tight perimeter with four-man positions, and hadn't seen any action in the area, so things seemed kind of okay. I situated the bed where I wanted it and was ready for the night.

After pulling the first hour of guard duty, I walked over and woke up the guy taking the next watch, then headed for my bed. Frank was already asleep, lying next to it on the ground. He'd let me know earlier what he thought about the bed; something about me needing my head examined. I lay down on it and quickly fell asleep.

Sometime later the sound of gunfire woke me. When I opened my eyes, .50 caliber tracers were cracking right over me as I lay there.

Holy Mackerel!

I tumbled off the bed, hitting the ground with a thud, and rolled under it. It was coming from behind us and kept on for a bit. Then it started coming from the trees far in front of us, going right over our position toward the trees behind. We were in the middle of crossfire.

After dark, the APCs had moved into the trees behind us. Charlie moved in across from them about 300 yards out. They began shooting at each other in the dark, not realizing we were in between. Bullets and tracers kept cracking over us from both directions.

Frank was quick to point out that I must have had about a minus-forty I.Q. to come up with such a bright idea about where and how to sleep. I believed him. If I had sat straight up, I would have gotten to go home—in a bag.

Lying on the ground seemed the safest thing to do. If we tried to move out, we could have been exposed. We lay there watching the gunfire go over us.

You never know where a good time will show up, and soon it all seemed funny. Frank and I got to laughing about the insanity of what was going on and couldn't stop. We even started joking about how stupid I was for lying up there on the little bed, as if I were at home.

"Oh, Mommy! They're shooting at us again! Would you make them stop?"

Frank was getting his digs in for some of the tricks I had pulled on him.

"Hey Bob, why don't you get back up on your little princess bed now? Those bullets can't hurt a stupid idiot like you!"

It was possible we were freaking out, with circumstances being just too heavy for us that night. This was one of the craziest situations we had been in. There wasn't much we could do but hope it would soon change for the better. Gradually, both sides stopped shooting at each other, and in the morning Charlie was nowhere to be found.

We were informed that we were going to get a four-day "Stand Down" after this operation. We hadn't been on one before, but knew that it meant we got to go somewhere safe and party. It seemed too good to be true.

The rain started again and lasted for six days straight with winds from 60 to 90 miles an hour. We were in a typhoon. We still walked around searching for the enemy, with the rain coming at us sideways. It was hard to make any kind of shelter at night because of the wind and rain. We were like wet rats out in that weather.

We headed back to the firebase. I was feeling weak, but managed to keep up because of the slow pace. We finally made it inside the base and started a fire with trip-flares and some big timbers we located.

I had never been cold in Vietnam before, but now I was shivering, feeling chills deep down inside. The fire felt good, but we soon heard a rumor claiming we couldn't stay inside the perimeter. That sounded crazy and I thought surely it couldn't be true. Why would our own guys kick us out in this terrible storm?

Sure enough, that afternoon we were ordered to move off the firebase. We were kicked out for some strange reason that no one would explain to us.

It was still raining hard and the winds had picked up. We humped out of the base and headed for a small hill about a mile away. By the time we got on top of the hill, it was almost dark. It was hard to stand in the wind and rain. The ground was rock hard, and most guys couldn't get any kind of shelter up. Steve and I managed to get two sticks in the ground and pulled our ponchos over them.

It was dark by then, and the winds were whipping us with hard rain. No perimeter was set up that night. We dropped our weapons in the mud and lay down next to them. There would be nobody on watch. If Charlie had it in him to come after us, it would be the best chance he would ever get.

Steve and I lay as close as we could get to each other, trying to keep warm. It was difficult to know what to do. It seemed as though the wind would blow us right off the hill. I don't know how we fell asleep, but we did.

When I woke up in the morning, five of us were lying there in a wet pile. Sometime during the night, others had joined Steve and me in an effort to find shelter of some sort.

As I untangled myself from the group, I looked over and saw Papa. He shook his head.

"I wouldn't treat a dog like this!" he said.

Our situation didn't make any sense to him either. In the morning light, the hill resembled a mud pile with a bunch of slugs on it. That was us: The Infantry, The Queen of Battle. We were treated like trash. I felt even more contempt for our upper echelon. The winds had been over 90 miles an hour that night.

We got ourselves together and moved off the hill and back into the firebase where we were assigned some bunkers and tents. The bunkers filled up quickly, so Gramps and I got one of the tents. We soon discovered that the wind had ripped the top out of it. We checked the others, but they had all been torn up, so we picked the one least damaged.

Gramps sat down, pulled my Buck knife out of his pack and started to whittle on a stick.

"Doggone you, Gramps! Where'd you get my knife this time?"

It seemed like every time I turned around he'd have something of mine. He seemed especially partial to the knife. Whenever I whined about him turning up with my stuff, he would start in on me about how I left my things lying along the trail.

"If it weren't for me pickin' up after you, Whitworth, you wouldn't have anything left in yer pack!"

I wasn't feeling very well and Gramps wasn't in top form either. He looked like he'd been rode hard and put away wet.

34

STAND DOWN

We moved to a firebase near the city of Chu Lai, where our company was directed into an empty wooden building with a big red cross painted on its roof, close to the post hospital. My platoon was put in formation outside and we were given some instructions on how to behave during our four-day break. I was standing up front, and then I wasn't.

Bam!

The ground had come up and hit me in the head.

I came to, lying in the dirt with my head spinning, and quickly passed out again. I woke up in the hospital. I had a thing about being in a hospital, but it was two days before they would release me. No one ever told me why I had collapsed.

I had very little strength, but walked the short distance across the base to the dilapidated Red Cross building.

It was the third day of Stand Down and the party had definitely started without me. When I stepped inside, two guys were chasing each other with the filthiest mop I had ever seen. They were so drunk they had no idea what they were doing as they took turns beating each other with it.

It was the middle of the day, and it looked as though I had missed two days of ludicrous chaos.

Wow!

A party like this was something I'd not yet experienced.

We were in a large abandoned hospital ward with bunk beds. There were beer cans, bottles, and trash strewn everywhere, with the two drunks stumbling all over. I went into the largest room where the whole company could gather. There was all the booze and soda anybody could drink. We had been promised a party and by the look of things, these guys had been hard at it.

There weren't many guys around, and I didn't know or care where everyone was. I was still low on energy and needed to take it easy. I didn't want the earth smacking me in the face again.

I found a quiet place and rested until evening and then went back to the big room where things were getting started. It was a large, open room with some tables and chairs set around. The ceiling was open and you could see the wooden rafters. Drinking was underway, and it looked like it was going to be another wild night.

A senior officer had shown up and was getting ready to speak to us. He was a tall, older man I hadn't seen before. He began telling us about our unit, some of the things we had done, and how proud he was of us. He said that someday in the far future we would have great stories to tell in the bars and that we should be proud of ourselves. He said how great we were and that he knew we were tough; we had been tough enough to make it for the months he sent us humping through the jungle and mountains in the rain.

I was getting angry listening to this blow-hard. There was nothing sincere in his talk. It sounded as if he had just shown up to let us know that he was high-ranking and could do anything he wanted with us. I had already seen how much some of these pencil-pushers would put us in harm's way just to make rank. I knew there were good officers, but he wasn't included with them. Papa's words on the rain-soaked hill still rang true in my ears: "I wouldn't treat a dog like this."

The guys in my platoon were great as far as I was concerned. They couldn't be given a party to match who they were. We were given the worst jobs day and night and had to face our greatest fears to do them. I was glad when this guy finished his spiel and left. I wasn't the only one who had quickly tired of his bloviating.

That night a Filipino band set up the gear for their show and soon began playing rock songs. Their lead singer was a small woman who danced around as she sang her heart out in accented English. Our captain, Six, who was a large strong man, sat in the first row smoking a big cigar and having a great time. After singing several songs, the little woman began a new one and jumped up on the captain's lap. She started dancing on his legs as he sat there puffing on his cigar. Things were off to a good start, and everybody was getting in on it.

Instead of drinking, I went to find some chow. There was lots of food for us, and I pigged out. I checked in on the party several hours later and most of the guys were pretty loaded. One guy was swinging from the rafters and dropped down into the crowd. There had been a few scuffles, but no real problems. When you're not drinking and everybody else is, watching them gets old pretty quick. The next day when you tell them what they were doing, they don't believe you.

I don't know how far into the wee hours those guys partied, but the following morning there was plenty of moaning as they woke up with hangovers. I was up before almost everyone.

The last day of Stand Down was pretty calm. Close to our area some choppers were parked next to a new Cobra gunship, the first of its type. We were glad to see this kind of firepower here to support us. It looked really mean. We took pictures of it to send home. That night there was another drink-fest, and I went in late to see what was happening. Everybody was having a good time and they were setting up for a movie, so I stayed to watch.

The movie got started, and it turned out to be a foreign porn-flick in black and white. There were two old naked people on the screen. I had never seen so much wrinkly skin. They looked to be in their eighties. I didn't know people that old could still have sex, much less want to; they looked too tired to try. I know there are bad movies, but this had to take the cake. I couldn't stomach watching any more, so I left. I would have needed to start drinking early in the day to watch that movie, but since drinking had never been a part of my life, I certainly wasn't going to start just for that.

35

TAM KY

After Stand Down was over, the platoon was fairly well-rested and somewhat partied out. We were taken to LZ Baldy where we patrolled the area again and guarded the mine-sweeping crews as they cleared the roads. This lasted a couple of weeks.

One afternoon when we came in from our daily patrol, I noticed that a BBQ grill was being set up. That was unusual. Soon word was out that we were going to get a big steak BBQ. That was great news, but...

Why were we going to be treated so well?

By now I had learned to question quickly. If something didn't seem okay, it paid to be alert to it right away. The steaks were great, and there were plenty of them, with other good food and drinks.

TAM KY: THE FIRST DAY
SEPTEMBER 21, 1968

The next morning lots of ammo showed up, and we were advised to help ourselves to it. Nobody said why, but we were ordered to be ready for an airlift. Plenty of choppers flew in to pick us up. The whole company was going on this maneuver. Still no word on where we were going. We loaded up and off we went.

Whup! Whup! Whup! Whup! Whup!

The big rotor turned as we rode through the air.

I always loved riding on choppers; it was cool looking down and out across the countryside.

Wouldn't it be wild fun, rabbit hunting from up here?

I could see some of my buddies on another chopper. They looked really rugged holding onto their rifles with grenades hanging off their pistol belts. It might have looked good, but being loaded with all that gear had gotten old a long time ago.

Where were we headed this time? Why the steak dinner and extra ammo?

That combination wasn't good.

As we came in low and set up to land, I saw three broken-up and burned choppers on the ground. It didn't look good and that uneasy feeling started settling in on me. Our choppers hovered a few feet above the ground so we could jump off.

When we hit the ground, our platoon headed off into the bush.

The area was hilly with lots of brush and trees. We searched the area for several hours looking for signs that Charlie had been there. Lots of things could give us a clue—like a cache of hidden supplies or small piles of ashes where he had warmed or cooked some food. We arrived at our destination and took a short break. I was then sent with a small patrol to check out some hills and valleys with plenty of cover. We returned without finding anything or making contact, which was fine with me. The rest of the company was around somewhere, but I had no idea where.

Our platoon had to get set up for the night and we had a hard time finding a good spot. Finally it was decided we would set up on a hill, even though it would be hard to defend. Spotter rounds were called in around our perimeter. After I pulled watch, I tried to find a level spot that was clear enough to put down my air mattress. I found a small area, pulled the mattress out of my rucksack, and blew into it. Then I put it on the ground in the dim dusk light and lay down.

Psssssssswoosh!

The mattress went flat.

What the heck? Had I put it on a sharp stick?

I sat up and jerked the thick tough material over and saw a two-inch hole. I looked closer at the ground underneath and saw big red ants scurrying out of their an ant hill. They had chewed that hole in the mattress in no time. I moved.

Soon after dark, flares started going off over our heads, lighting up the whole area as if it were daytime. One of the firebases was covering us with them. They shot artillery rounds that carried the flares high up into the air where they popped. Small chunks of steel fell from the sky as the flares were released to slowly drift down under what looked like small parachutes while they lit up the sky. The steel chunks from the artillery rounds came crashing down through the brush all night long. I was worried that they would fall on me while I tried to sleep through the wearisome night.

This place was strange: crashed and burned helicopters, flares at night, and no Charlie anywhere.

What were we in for?

I absolutely asked for God's care over each of the guys that night.

TAM KY: THE SECOND DAY
SEPTEMBER 22, 1968

In the morning, our captain sent Third Platoon to patrol the same area we had searched for NVA the afternoon before. Their lieutenant had the platoon break into squads and move in a cloverleaf formation through the valley. Shortly after they moved into the trees, they hit heavy resistance and started taking casualties.

Our platoon was sent up onto the ridge overlooking the valley as backup. We could hear gunfire coming from the trees and it didn't sound good. I was at the end of the ridge with one of the new guys recently infused into our platoon. He was chomping at the bit to get into the fight and was mad because we had been sent up here as backup. The last guy I knew who'd been in a hurry to get into a gunfight was dead in no time, so this guy's attitude was worrisome at best. I listened to his ranting, but had nothing to say to him. He sounded like he had more guts than brains.

Lt. Dennis called me up front and pointed out three running figures that were about 1,100 yards away from where the fight was raging. I watched them disappear under a tree. The lieutenant handed me an M72 LAW rocket.

No way! I would need a lucky shot for sure!

I looked behind me to make sure no one was standing there to catch the blast, then pulled the pins, slid out the inner tube until it locked into place, and set the LAW on my shoulder. Guessing on a line of sight, I pointed it up high, looked through the small sight, and squeezed on the trigger.

Boom!

It fired with a loud blast. We all watched as the rocket flew so high that we almost lost sight of it. Then it started dropping.

It seemed to take forever. The rocket picked up speed as it fell, dropped straight through the tree, and exploded. We had seen three figures run under that tree, now only one ran out.

Some of our guys let out a loud shout. I couldn't believe I had slopped the shot in!

We were up on the ridge waiting for hours. We could see NVA soldiers with backpacks on, carrying AK47s, and running their strange duck-walk stride far out in front of us, but they were so quick getting to cover that we couldn't get any effective shots off. We had to be careful where we shot because Third Platoon was down there in the heavy terrain somewhere and the last thing they needed was friendly fire coming from us. As time went on, air strikes were called in.

We found out later that one of the captain's RTOs was killed by sniper fire, and Third Platoon had been shot up quite badly. They had one KIA and several wounded, including the sergeant who earlier had shown such bad judgment. He had been shot where it would affect his heritage.

TAM KY: THE THIRD DAY
SEPTEMBER 23, 1968

Most of the details of these days, September 21-25, are indelibly etched in my mind. On the morning of this particular day, First Platoon rescued one of their soldiers whose squad had been ambushed by NVA the night before. After the ambush, the enemy went into the area and killed one of our soldiers who had been wounded. The guy who was rescued had faked being dead all night while the NVA soldiers camped beside him.

But some things, especially on this day, are shrouded in vagueness. I know that at some point our company loaded on APCs and tanks, and rode for the better part of the day.

When we unloaded in the evening, we were in Quang Ngai Province near Tam Ky. The terrain was mostly flat, with rice paddies as far as you could see. Hills, clumps of trees, and villages were scattered throughout the area. We set up in the middle of a rice paddy.

There were companies of ARVNs gathered in the area. It was obvious that there would be some kind of operation happening the next day and they were there to help. I watched as South Vietnamese propeller-driven airplanes dive-bombed a heavily treed area. From a high altitude, each plane dove straight down releasing its bomb. I could hear the deafening roar of the air-crafts as they descended toward their targets. The planes made several passes and then lifted.

It was fascinating to watch those dive-bombers. It was the first time I had seen them at work.

I still had no idea what we would be up against, but it was obvious we were gearing up for something big.

TAM KY: THE FOURTH DAY
SEPTEMBER 24, 1968

The next morning I looked around and there were no ARVN soldiers to be seen anywhere.

Why aren't they here? Where had they all gone? This whole deal was spooky.

More APCs and tanks had shown up. I had never seen so many in one location. Other well-armed infantry companies I hadn't seen before were also there setting up. The APCs and tanks were getting lined up horizontally, facing a long line of 40-foot-high trees about 150 yards out in front, and stretching endlessly away from us to the right. We still hadn't been informed about what was ahead of us, but this was looking deadly serious.

There was no indication of what was waiting out there in the trees. The statement "ignorance is bliss" was about to take on a whole new meaning. We were ordered to leave our rucksacks and get on-line between the tanks and tracks, which meant that two or three of us were to stand between each vehicle. We were forming a powerful line of armor.

Steve and I, with hand grenades and M16s, were between two APCs. The line lunged forward, firing everything it had into the trees. I had never seen so much gunfire! Each track was firing all three of its machine guns at once. The tanks were rapidly firing their heavy guns, with each of their machine guns spewing solid lines of fire into the tree line. On foot, we grunts were firing our M16s or M60s at everything out in front of us. At the same time, enemy gunfire and Rocket Propelled Grenades were coming back at us from the tree line. I had never seen anything like this. An "RPG" was generally able to penetrate the steel on a tank and explode, scattering shrapnel to wound or kill those inside. A track had less protection, and an RPG would always blow right through it, melting the metal like butter to unleash its deadly charge.

We were moving into a battle more ferocious than I had ever contemplated. As we moved forward, bullets were everywhere, ripping right past us from the tree line. I couldn't believe that Steve and I weren't being hit. We glanced at each other at the same time. Steve had a look of total amazement on his face.

How were all of these bullets missing us?

This seemed way beyond luck. The noise was deafening as we continued walking and firing into the trees.

A dink popped up out of a spider hole about 30 feet in front of us with an RPG on his shoulder. I could hardly believe my eyes. How could anybody have guts enough to pop up in front of that much gunfire? He fired the rocket our way, then quickly dropped back down into his hole. It barely missed us as it screamed by. It was then that I realized we were bigger targets than he had been.

The area in front of us was solid red tracer fire. We kept moving forward with all the bullets cracking past us. Steve and I kept glancing at each other in total disbelief that we were actually walking in a completely out in the open, on-line assault into enemy fire. It was nuts!

Whap!

I was hit!

I had a sharp pain just above my knee. I dropped back to the side of the track and took a look at my leg.

Dang!

It was just a small piece of shrapnel about a half-inch deep. No going in on the chopper with just that. I needed to ignore it.

Shortly after, the APCs stopped moving forward because they had been hit with so much enemy fire. The enemy in the tree line was dug in very well. I assumed it was the NVA we were finally fighting. They were the Big League. They would never dig in and fight with us unless they were well prepared and fighting on their terms. I had a much higher respect for them than the VC thugs. The VC were terrorists who would hit and run, ambush us, and torture their own people. They wouldn't stay and fight like a disciplined army. The enemy in the trees seemed well prepared. They must have believed they stood a good chance of taking us, because they stayed and shelled out a tremendous amount of firepower. They were betting their lives they could beat us. But whenever there was a battle like this, we brought such firepower that it meant they would pay a heavy price.

Steve called it the "Walk of Death." We backed farther away from the trees to regroup and take care of our wounded.

How had we not been killed?

Some of the armor had been hit with rockets, but I didn't know how many or what casualties there were.

I sat down next to Frank on a patch of lush green grass under some broad-leafed bushes. We were sitting close in this shady little garden, believing we were hidden from sight by the big leaves. It was nice and cool in this small spot of tranquility next to the battlefield. We were talking about the situation when automatic weapons fire ripped through the leaves, hitting the dirt between us. We rolled away from each other and took off running for better cover. How had that guy spotted us?

When we regrouped about an hour later, the armor got back on-line, and we received orders to get in front of the armored tracks. Did someone think we were bullet proof? Once again, it gave me the unwanted feeling of being expendable. When the tracks started moving forward and the shooting started again, I was ten feet in front of Steve, who was a few feet in front of Gary. We were on the right end of the line of armor heading across the paddy toward a small hill.

It was insanity all over again. RPGs and way too many bullets went flying past us. Suddenly, an RPG went just past my head on the right.

BOOM!

It hit the track right behind Gary. About 400 yards to the right, I saw another APC burning with smoke streaming from it. I looked back and saw Gary on the ground. He had taken shrapnel in his upper back from the RPG when it hit the track, and the blast had blown him to the ground. I would soon realize how extremely fortunate he had been when I witnessed the brutal killing of someone else by the same type of hit.

We got Gary back to cover and the tracks pulled back as well. Other wounded men were being brought to the same location to be picked up by a descending medevac chopper. And then...

BOOOOOM!

The biggest explosion I had ever seen sent smoke billowing straight up 500 feet to make a huge mushroom cloud. Behind me, the back door of a track went flying past. The door was four feet wide and could have taken out six or eight guys with no problem! At the same time a four-way lug wrench propellered across in front of me. Pieces of metal were flying everywhere! The chopper was hit by the huge blast, causing it to jerk and wobble as the pilot fought to land.

I thought that the Russians must have given the NVA some small nukes that they were firing from up on the hill next to us. For a few terrified minutes after that huge explosion, I thought we might lose this fight. Then someone informed us that the explosion came from hundreds of pounds of C-4 that was on board the burning track to my right. At the same time the explosion went off, the Medevac finally landed next to us, and we rushed to put Gary and the others who were wounded on as fast as we could. Some of them were shot up badly and didn't look like they would make it. We filled the chopper with wounded men and it quickly flew out of sight.

Thirty-five years later, I told this story to a group of local combat vets.

"I was there."

It was Stephen, a pipeline welder who occasionally came to the group.

You've got to be kidding! How could someone here have been there at Tam Ky?

"Did you see the explosion?" I asked.

"Yes, I was the crew chief on the Medevac that came to pick up your wounded. As we flew in, the pilot had seen how fierce the fighting was and radioed down that he didn't think he could land. Someone came back over the radio as we were trying to figure the best way in and said, 'Land or you'll be shot down.' "

Stephen went on. "As we were about to set down, we got new orders to abort our landing immediately. That was when the explosion blew us sideways, as chunks of shrapnel hit the chopper. My left arm was cut from shrapnel and my M16 was damaged. The clip on it was so badly bent that the rifle wouldn't function. Then, in our effort to get your wounded to the hospital, the pilot put so much power to the chopper after take-off, that it had been seriously damaged and needed to be repaired."

I was dumbfounded to hear Stephen's account of that experience. It was 100% right on.

The last thing I remember about that day was that it was almost dark when we moved out. I got on the last track to leave the area and it didn't want to stay running. It looked as though we were going to be left behind. But we managed to catch up and all the tracks pulled back from the battleground and formed a large circle.

The track-gunners pulled watch all that night and I got to sleep down inside, lying on a rucksack and a five-gallon gas can. There were mosquitoes buzzing around and light rain falling, but I found a way to stay kind of dry. After enduring that battle alongside Steve and the others, I could have slept anywhere.

Neither of the on-line assaults I had been on that day had made it into the enemy's position. The NVA were still out there, reinforcing their troops and waiting for us. At that point, I didn't know who was winning or losing, nor did I know much about who had been killed or wounded. I knew we had shoved some seriously wounded men on the Medevac.

It had been a frightful day—and there was more to come.

When I prayed, I knew to ask that He give me the wherewithal to take it, and the inner-strength to stand—no matter what happened.

"Jesus, please be with us."

Never before had I depended so much on my prayers.

TAM KY: THE FIFTH DAY
SEPTEMBER 25, 1968

The next morning the APCs and tanks lined up next to each other again with about 10 to 15 feet between them. As they moved into position, I noticed a tank I had seen the day before stuck so far down in the rice paddy that the mud almost reached its big gun turret. I looked more closely and saw a small round hole smack in the front on the farthest right side where an RPG had penetrated deep into the metal. Soldiers were working around it trying to get it to move, but it was just spinning its big tracks and not going anywhere.

We were at the far left end of the armor line, waiting to go. Someone walked over to me after talking to Jerry and asked if I knew where he could get a couple of guys to operate machine guns on the last two tracks at this end of the line. Not wanting to be out in the open anymore, and not alert or smart enough to ask what had happened to the missing gunners, I stepped over to Frank.

"The track guys need two gunners. Let's run the '60s for them."

"Sure," he said with his little grin—like we had just lucked out.

Frank got on the very last track to the left and I climbed on the one next to him. The M60 he was to operate was on the right side of his track and my gun was on the left side of mine, so we could look right at each other. I worked the bolt on my gun and it was dry. I looked through the track for some gun oil. The only thing I found was an open quart can of 30-weight motor oil. There was no time to break the gun apart for a good cleaning, so I opened the bolt and poured oil on the action and cycled it a few times. It seemed okay, so I loaded the ammo belt and was ready to go.

The troops were ready to go too, standing behind the armor all the way down the row. So far, this engagement had been very scary. That awful feeling I got when I thought things may not go well was there in my belly.

There's no getting out of this.

The day before was the only time I had ever seen someone so cowardly that he faked an injury, ran for the medevac chopper, and dived on with the wounded. Heck, we'd all wanted on that chopper, but there was no way that we would leave each other alone in this mess. We had a tough job to do and were in it together.

That was the real reason Steve and I had walked out there yesterday where the bullets and rockets were cracking and blasting past us. We cared about each other and were looking out for one another. This morning, we were worried about what the day might hold for each of us.

I thought back to when that little girl had told us the children were leaving her village. Thanks to her and Gary we'd made it out of there just in time. I remembered all the friendly fire, the shrapnel from the grenade that had cut my face, the hospital being mortared, the land mines that had killed two of our guys, and the others who had gotten lost or walked point and ended up dead. There had been the grenade that hadn't killed Jerry and me, and the gunfire that Steve and I had walked through the day before, and all the near misses and situations that could have been called "coincidences" when those in my platoon were not killed.

That night four months earlier in the bunker, I had asked God to watch over the guys in my platoon and not let any more of them die. Now, here we were facing the most dangerous fight we had been in. I didn't know what to expect in the days ahead, but if it was going to be anything like yesterday, it would be brutal.

The word to go must have come over the radio to the track

commanders, because the entire line of tracks surged forward like a tidal wave. We moved across the rice paddies, heading for a hedgerow about 300 yards in front of us. Our whole long line of armor opened fire with everything it had. We had solid tracer fire out in front of us again.

When we hit the hedgerow, we rolled right over the bushes, roaring forward. As we passed trees, it looked as though every leaf had bullet holes in it. We passed by a dead water buffalo. He had been shot so many times that it looked as though you could dip a knife in him and spread his flesh on a piece of bread like mincemeat.

We made it through this area in short order and dropped down into the rice paddies again. We hadn't hit any resistance and were still going like crazy. We made it through the paddies and over the next hedgerow into more trees and bushes; there was still no resistance. We fired at everything. I glanced over at Frank and he seemed to be having a good time hunched down behind his machine gun laying out a red line of fire as we roared ahead.

We broke back into paddies again, and as we moved forward into the middle, my M60 quit firing. It still had plenty of ammo so I worked the action a few times, but the gun wouldn't fire. I tried a couple more times but it was a no-go. The next hedgerow was coming up fast, so I grabbed my M16 and began firing. We went through the hedgerow, some bushes, and into a small clearing on higher ground. Fifteen feet to my right the clearing ended. Tall trees partially covered the rest of the armored vehicles that were continuing their attack from positions just short of the rice paddies ahead.

A loud explosion shook me. I looked to my left and realized an RPG had hit Frank's track, stopping it instantly. Then the track I was in came to a sudden halt. We were just in front and 10 feet to the right of Frank's track. The next hedgerow was about 50 feet in front of us and curved around to the left for about 30 feet on that side. As I turned to my left, I could see a short L-shaped dirt bunker coming out about 15 feet in front of the hedgerow. I watched as Frank and the crew shot out of their track like lightning, and it looked as if Frank was dragging someone with him. They disappeared behind me into the trees where the battle raged on.

Bullets started flying everywhere, hitting the track, and cracking past me. I was facing the bunker head on. Instantly, 15 NVA soldiers burst out of the left side of the hedgerow and came running my way. We usually encountered the enemy when they were hiding in the hedgerows, bushes, and trees as they sniped at us, ambushed us, set off mines, and did anything they could to kill or wound us while we couldn't see them. Now here they were, right in front of me.

Some of them broke off to the left through the bushes and small trees. One soldier was headed straight at me as fast as he could run. He was dressed in a green uniform, had black hair, and was staring at me with huge, panic-filled eyes. His mouth was wide open—screaming—but I couldn't hear him because of all the gunfire. His face was full of terror, showing he expected to be killed at any moment.

In a second he was five feet in front of me. Then he swerved to my left and darted between the tracks. This was crazy! They were all headed straight for our forces behind me in the trees and would be dead in no time.

Was I going to stay and fight?

It felt like a switch flipped inside me. I picked a guy that ran to my right. He jumped into a trench and could only run straight away. It looked as though he was going 70 miles an hour, but that didn't matter, I knew I had him dead to rights. As I turned, I snapped the M16 up to my shoulder, placed the sights on his spine about three inches below his neck, and squeezed the trigger. In my mind's eye I could already see him falling.

Click.

My rifle was empty. He kept running.

No way! I don't believe this!

When an M16 was empty, the bolt stayed open so you could see you needed to reload, but that hadn't happened. My brain felt like it had stripped a gear.

My mind flashed back to the time I'd had a chance to kill the VC a few months earlier. I remembered him standing in front of Gary and me; how I aimed not to kill. At that moment, the image of my bullet ripping through him, knocking him to the ground, was too harsh. I didn't have it in me. It would have been too huge a leap to kill someone standing right in front of me. Since then, however, things had changed and I was now able to do it without hesitation.

I quickly shoved a full clip in my rifle and turned back toward the bunker. Bullets were still coming from everywhere.

As I looked into the distance, I could see a hooch about 60 yards past the hedgerow in the left part of the rice paddy area. It was hard to see, but it seemed like some of the gunfire was coming from there.

Just then, I realized someone was coming up behind me, heading diagonally between Frank's track and mine. Third Platoon had gotten shot up pretty badly two days before, so I was surprised to see it was Mark from that platoon, carrying an M60 machine gun. I wondered how he had gotten here so quickly; I thought we had left all the grunts way behind when our tracks moved out so fast.

Mark had no idea what danger he was in. As he came around the corner of my track, I leaned out, yelling as loud as I could.

"Stay back! Stay back! Stay back!"

But the gunfire was so loud he couldn't hear me. Then I leaned out as far as I could, and tried to grab him.

"Stay back!"

I kept yelling at the top of my voice.

I couldn't reach him; I missed grabbing him by about six inches. He never saw or heard me. He moved ahead, firing the machine gun as he walked. He was shot and fell to the ground directly in front of the bunker. I didn't know how hard he had been hit, but he was not moving at all.

Bullets were still coming close; I could hear them crack as they passed my head and shoulder, some hitting the track. I shot into the bushes and hedgerow on the far side of the bunker, but couldn't see where the gunfire was actually coming from. It looked like the guy who shot Mark had to be right in front of me. I kept cramming ammo into my rifle, firing at anything that could have been a hiding place. Then I noticed someone else coming the same way Mark had come. It was the Third Platoon medic.

"No! No! Stop! Stop!"

I yelled as loud as I could, while forcing myself up and over the edge of the track, almost falling out onto the ground. I was waving my arms, reaching for him, and screaming.

"Stay back! Stay back! Stay back! Stop!!!"

He just kept walking straight toward Mark, as if he didn't know I was there. He wasn't carrying a rifle; he had nothing to protect himself. I watched in a daze. When he reached Mark, he knelt down and put his hand on Mark's neck to check his pulse.

After a few seconds he stood up, turned around, and walked back to where Frank's blown track was sitting. There he paused and turned around to look back at Mark lying on the ground by the bunker. He was standing about 10 feet to my left. Right when I thought he was going to make it, an RPG was fired from the hedgerow bushes and slammed into the front of the track, just missing his head. The shrapnel and blast from the rocket hit him in the back of his head. He jerked forward and fell to the ground as the concussion passed through me.

I was stunned from the blast and don't know how much time passed. The next thing I remember seeing was a light reflecting off something in the hedgerow behind the bunker.

Then a dark, shadowy figure moved into position to fire his RPG launcher. Pulling my rifle to my shoulder, I fired one shot and he dropped out of sight. I didn't know if he was dead or wounded, but I wasn't taking any chances.

I turned and dropped down inside the track, looking for hand grenades. That's when I realized I was alone. I wondered where the track crew had gone.

Why they had left? Was I the only guy fighting this fight?

Well, there was no time to think about that. Bullets started hitting the side of the track in rapid succession, but weren't penetrating its interior. I found a grenade and stood up on the edge of a bench fastened to the inside wall.

As I came up out of the track, the bullets stopped. I held the handle of the grenade and pulled the pin. I had to throw it just over the edge of the hedgerow. If it went too far it would land in the rice paddy and not have the needed effect. If I didn't throw it far enough, it would land in front of the bunker and kill Mark, if he was still alive.

It was a short distance, about 35 feet. I threw the grenade. It landed two feet past Mark, on the crown of the bunker where it wobbled back and forth. I couldn't believe my eyes! It looked as though it was going to roll down on Mark!

There was no doubt if it stayed where it was, or rolled back next to him, he would be dead for sure. If that happened, I would lose my mind. The sudden shock of that real possibility sent a wave of horror over me. Seconds passed but it seemed like eternity. Finally, the grenade slowly rolled down the other side of the bunker and exploded.

All this time there was still gunfire everywhere; the bullets just weren't hitting me.

I dropped back down into the track, looking for more grenades. While I was looking, bullets slammed into the side of track again. Charlie must have emptied his 30-round clip on the track because when I stood up the bullets stopped.

How many NVA were out there?

I kept looking for these guys but still couldn't spot anyone. I jerked the pin on the grenade and threw—this time harder. It landed just past the hedgerow.

Duck.

Explosion!

Back down inside the track.

The grenades were getting harder to find in the midst of all the debris. Hundreds of empty shell casings, old paperback books, a bulky rucksack, full and empty ammo cans, water canteens, various tools, rags, and junk were all over the floor. My head was about a foot from the wall of the track and I could hear the bullets slamming hard against the track's side. If the hull had been any thinner, I would have taken them right in my skull.

Why doesn't he wait until I stand up and just shoot me? Isn't he taking any shrapnel from the grenades?

I found another grenade, and when I stood up again the bullets stopped. I couldn't believe it. I pulled the pin and threw. This one landed okay.

Duck.

Explosion!

Back down inside, I could find only one more grenade. I knew I was going to need more, but this was it. I stood up, pulled the pin, threw the grenade, and bent over quickly.

Explosion!

I grabbed my rifle and stood back up, but this time I jumped, lifting myself up on a small ledge, diagonally behind the M60, next to the .50 caliber machine-gun turret. The M60 had a shield in front of it for protecting the shooter, but I was somewhat above the shield, exposing more of my body, as I tried to spot the guy with the AK47. My eyes frantically searched through the bushes and small trees but I couldn't see anyone. Bullets slammed rapidly against the shield and ricocheted away.

I knew these guys liked full-auto, but why didn't he just switch it to semi, take aim, and shoot me? He had to be pretty close. Everything was hitting the shield.

Why didn't even one bullet hit me?

I felt a tranquil peace surround me.

"You're participating in a miracle," I heard.

The peace lasted only a few moments.

Did I really hear that?

The bullets stopped, so I figured his 30-round clip was empty again, and jumped down off the track. I ran toward the line of armor to get more grenades and saw one of the captain's RTOs kneeling in the bushes, holding his rifle, and looking at me. I ran over to him.

"You got grenades?"

"No."

I moved on and found someone who did. I now had four grenades and headed back to the track. As I walked around in front, I switched my rifle to full auto and fired into the hedgerow as I moved forward. My rifle was so hot it would hardly fire. I felt as though I was in "No-man's land"—"the kill zone."

I had no illusions as to what would happen to me if I were hit by enemy fire. My belly was knotted in anguish. I didn't have far to go. I kept firing until I made it to Mark. I leaned past him and threw some grenades into the bunker opening. Then I grabbed his shirt collar at the back of his neck and leaned down to my left as the grenades exploded much louder than I had expected.

I started pulling Mark back away from the bunker. He was heavy, and I had a hard time dragging him while staying low and firing into the hedgerow at the same time. As I struggled to move him back, I felt someone's hand on my shoulder.

Who in their right mind would come out here?

I glanced up.

There stood Frank. Empty-handed, no weapon or helmet,

just a big target. I could see bloodstained holes in his pants.

Never had I ever been so happy. Seeing Frank with all his courage, having him touch my arm, made me feel like I wasn't alone and gave me something I had lost. I didn't know what Frank knew about the danger we were in, but he could see things had gotten worse since he left. He had not hesitated to come out and help.

Without saying a word, Frank reached down, picked Mark up in his arms, and started back toward the tracks, fully exposed. I stood up, firing into the hedgerow and bushes as I backed away, trying to cover us. When we got behind my track, Frank gently laid Mark on the ground. I went to where the medic lay, kneeled down and picked him up.

Why had Charlie fired the RPG at him and not me?

I carried him back and put him down beside Mark.

Frank and I looked Mark over and it was plain to see by his wounds that he had been killed when he was first shot. The medic almost looked okay, but I had been so close when the RPG struck, I knew how hard he had been hit from behind.

Things were quieting down. Now that the shooting was letting up, I noticed a very loud ringing in my ears. An ex-NVA soldier, a "Kit Carson Scout" now working with us, showed up and went behind the hedgerow where most of the bullets and RPGs had come from. It was the same place that I had thrown the four grenades.

He came back with a loaded, brand-new-looking, green, Russian-made, RPG launcher with an optical sight. He handed it to me and left. Other GIs started to show up and I wondered where they had all come from. I handed them the launcher and they started working to get it unloaded.

I walked over to look behind the hedgerow to see where the grenades had landed. On the way, in the bushes, I saw a dead NVA soldier who looked as though he had just laid down and died. His dark eyes seemed to stare at me as I passed by.

I stepped behind the hedgerow and smelled raw torn flesh. I glanced forward and saw the mangled body of an NVA soldier lying next to the second opening of the L-shaped bunker. It was a terrible sight; all four grenades had landed on him. I was worried about sniper fire coming from the other side of the rice paddies, so I quickly stepped back behind the hedgerow and walked around to the bunker where Mark had been shot.

The guys had removed the rocket from the launcher, dismantled it, and taken off the optical sight by then. The bunker had caved in from the blast of the grenades I'd thrown in. It was so badly damaged, I wondered if some of their ordnance had been set off. I walked over to the opening and pulled out four dead NVA soldiers. Their bodies were in really bad shape. I looked back toward where the RPG was, but the guys had left with it. I had wanted to keep the telescopic sight, but I was so happy to be alive I wasn't too concerned about it.

The images of the wounds of the men hit and the horrid condition of the bodies after the fight seared into my mind, never to be shared. The details serve no purpose, except to glimpse the horror of battle, or show the price that had been exacted from the men who had sacrificed all.

I was beginning to think it was finally over, but I was all jacked up inside. I noticed someone working hard on Third Platoon's medic. He was kneeling next to him between the two tracks, giving him mouth-to-mouth; making every effort to bring him back.

I needed to calm down and didn't know what to do so I looked for some C-rations. Even though I wasn't hungry, it had been a long time since I had eaten. I found some in the track and Frank and I sat down next to the blown bunker and opened the rations. When Frank's track had been hit with the first RPG, one soldier had been killed, two seriously wounded, and Frank's legs had been hit with shrapnel. I was very thankful that he had ignored his wounds and returned to help me.

Bruce, who hadn't been in on this fight, walked up to me. "What are you doing?"

"Eating peaches," I replied.

I don't think that was the answer he was expecting; he could see the dead lying on the ground behind us.

I heard jets coming in very close. Evidently, the NVA who had lived through the battle had pulled back across the paddies about 100 yards away. The air strike was aimed at them.

The jets lined up for their drop and I lost sight of Frank as he and I ran for cover. I hid behind a large tree, but was still too close when the bombs hit; the huge blasts sent dirt and shrapnel flying everywhere. I looked for better cover but couldn't move anywhere safely. The air strikes' numerous blasts were deafening. When the bombs hit, shrapnel went screaming through the tree limbs above me, and dirt kept falling all around. Fortunately, the strikes didn't last long.

Soldiers had brought six or seven more KIAs and left their bodies beside Mark and the medic. It was time for me to try to find my squad. As I walked past the tracks, I could see that it was the lieutenant from Third Platoon still feverishly trying to resuscitate the medic. I didn't have it in me to tell him how hard he had been hit. I was empty and had nothing left to give.

I was low on ammo, so I walked over to a large pile of ammunition that I had seen being pushed out of a hovering chopper earlier in the fight. I put two 100-round belts of M60 ammo across my shoulders along with a 180-round bandolier of M16 bullets. I hoped this was over, but I didn't know for sure that it was. I kept walking until I spotted Jerry and Fred.

As I approached, a person with a camera, who looked to me like a news reporter, took my picture.* I sure didn't feel friendly and I probably didn't look it. It had been a bitter day of failure, death, and regret so far, and I despised the press for the way they were representing us. He never said a word to me.

*Cover photo and page 211

I walked over to Jerry.

"Did you guys hit any trouble?" I asked.

"Not much," he answered. "What about you?"

I couldn't describe what I had been through, so I just told him we had hit some action down on the end. I felt exhausted.

Shortly after, we were given orders to do one more push out to the front. Jerry wanted me to work with the guy shooting the M60, but I was done for the day. I was slowly realizing what I had just survived and was thoroughly shaken. Jerry couldn't have known what was going on inside me, but he could see something wasn't right and gave me a much-needed break.

Sometime later, it was all over. All of us grunts loaded on the tracks and left. As I looked back over the rice paddies, I could see the terrible damage that had been done to the land.

I never found out how many men were killed or wounded with the armor or other infantry units. My company had at least six Killed-In-Action, but I didn't know how many were wounded. It was reported that we had been fighting over 1,000 well-armed NVA soldiers who had sustained over 400 "KIAs," and countless more wounded.

My platoon had some wounded, but no deaths. Some of the guys had heard that Frank and I were killed when the tracks got hit with rockets. It was hard for me to grasp how I had come through the last two days with only a small wound in my leg. I ignored the wound and never had it treated. It was the least of my worries.

We rode the tracks for hours and ended up on a hill somewhere. After we had been there awhile, I saw a chopper coming in. I approached the landing site where ponchos covered the men who had been killed earlier. When the chopper set down, the rotor-wash blew the ponchos off their bodies.

A chaplain, with a grin on his face and smoking a big cigar, got off the chopper. When he saw the bodies, he was stunned. It looked like he was overwhelmed with what he saw. Although chaplains usually came into the field to come alongside and encourage the soldiers, this man arrived unprepared to meet men who were battle-worn. He hurriedly walked away and returned a few minutes later. The cigar was gone and so was his grin. He got back on the chopper, and it took off. I was not surprised at his reaction.

I recognized this particular chaplain because I had spoken with him when we'd first arrived in-country. I hadn't been doing very well with the whole "killing" thing. I had made some adjustments to my thinking in training when I heard an admonition from one of the old sergeants.

"Always kill the enemy. He might not kill you, but he could kill your buddy."

That sunk in deeply, but my mind still hadn't crossed over. At that stage, it was hard getting used to the reality of killing someone. There was nothing easy about that, so when we were in the rear I had gone to talk to this chaplain about killing. He didn't seem to know the Bible and had no insight for me. Being a chaplain was just a job to him.

A short time after that encounter, another chaplain came out to the field and I had a chance to have a straight talk with him. He understood our circumstances, what we had to do, and that we carried a heavy load. He knew God's Word and spent time answering my questions. He cared about and was concerned for us.

Now the empty chaplain had come to us on the chopper with nothing to give. After seeing his reaction, I knew I wanted to have something to benefit others in a time of need. I would do my best to tell anyone who asked me where it was I got my hope.

Bob on the fifth day at Tam Ky.

Photo by Dana Stone, Associated Press

I would have lost heart,
unless I had believed that
I would see the goodness of the Lord
in the land of the living.
Wait on the Lord; be of good courage,
and He shall strengthen your heart.
Wait on the Lord.
Psalm 27:13-14

36

MALARIA

I woke up standing in the dark with a pistol in my hand. This was the third time I had awakened while sleepwalking at night. Fortunately we were at a firebase, but this was worrisome.

Why had I started doing this? Could I somehow stop it?

I hadn't been feeling top-notch since the battle and didn't know how long we would be at this firebase before we moved out.

A few days later I was informed that for some reason a few of us were going to be given medals. That didn't make much sense to me.

We were given a clean shirt to wear but not clean pants. Some of us from Second Platoon were ordered to stand in formation with some other soldiers.

Soon an officer showed up and we were put at attention. He and his assistant began walking down the line, pinning medals to our clean shirts. I felt embarrassed.

Why were medals being pinned on just some of us, when other men in our platoon had faced their fears in battle and also fought with honor? Why weren't all of us being recognized for our service? We'd all been in that terrible battle a couple of weeks earlier, and serving our country was the duty of us all.

That last day when I had encountered the enemy was the worst, but I didn't think anyone had witnessed what took place.

What was so special about me?

I was sent here to fight and didn't like being singled out.

... And what was the deal with the clean shirt but dirty pants? I guess the guy didn't really care about what we wore as long as he didn't have to touch any of the filth associated with the reality of our daily lives.

While we were still on the firebase, I began running a fever. I was sent to a hospital in Da Nang. When I checked in I was told to get bedding from a sectioned-off area. As I headed over there, I gestured for some from a young orderly standing behind a half door.

"What's your name?" he asked.

"B-B-B-B."

"What's your name?" he asked again.

"B-B-B-B."

We went back and forth like this several times before he reached over and slapped me across the face. It took me by surprise! What a shock!

"What's your name?"

"Bob!"

I was amazed! I wanted to say, "Thanks, I needed that," but was feeling too poorly.

I was put to bed and, after a blood test, was diagnosed with malaria. I slept for a full day while my fever kept rising. Sluggishly coming to my senses, I looked over at the fellow in the next bed. When he turned toward me I could see that the whites of his eyes were solid blood red. He was delirious.

"I'm a Marine," he managed to say. "I have malaria." His voice was very weak. "There were three other Marines in that bed before you who died from the same thing."

Well, that was encouraging.

I was informed if my fever reached 106 degrees they would have to take measures to cool me off. It wasn't long before they brought in a large flat rubber mat. They wrapped it around me and started pumping it full of ice-cold water. I was freezing and already shaking with the chills. They had to be careful or I would get pneumonia and that could end it all.

A week later, I stabilized and was flown south to a large recovery center in Cam Rahn Bay where I stayed almost three weeks. By the time I was discharged, I'd lost 23 pounds off my normal weight of 180, which made me feel scrawny and weak.

Having nothing with me but the clothes I'd worn, I caught a ride on a C-130 aircraft to somewhere about 150 miles north, and then hitched a ride on a Huey heading for Chu Lai.

When I got on the chopper, things started to liven up. The pilot and crew were up for a good time. The pilot put the chopper about 50 feet above the road we were following, going as fast as it could fly. He was buzzing everything and everyone below us.

After a while he pulled up a couple hundred feet and put the chopper out over the rice paddies. One of the crew produced a box of hand grenades and it was suddenly like the Fourth of July! Grenade after grenade was thrown from the chopper, exploding in midair while the pilot zigzagged through the territory.

When the grenades were used up, out came some "Willy Peter" or white phosphorous grenades. Those grenades were larger and heavier, and when they went off, a shower of white streaming smoke filled the air. We put on quite a show, leaving a smoky trail behind us. These guys weren't afraid to let off a little steam! I was getting a wild ride back and loving every minute of it.

We landed at the Chu Lai airport near where I had to report in. I would need to find my unit the next day. I headed for a place to hang out and was glad to find a soda and some nuts. That was all that was available besides some pickled pigs' feet.

It was getting dark so I located an old empty building near some artillery guns. I lay down on the wooden floor and quickly fell asleep. I awoke in the middle of the night to the artillery battery firing a mission. I was sick, with a splitting headache, and began throwing up. It didn't take long and I was dry heaving. I had never had the dry heaves before and they wouldn't stop.

I started off to find an aid station. It was the middle of the night and I had no idea where to find help. I made my way to a main road and waited, hoping someone would come along. I was heaving and getting sicker. I heard a jeep coming in the dark and bummed a ride. I was dropped off at an aid station and went inside looking for assistance.

There was an orderly behind the desk and I told him I was sick.

"What unit are you from?" he asked.

"Fourth and Twenty-first Infantry," I replied.

"Sorry, can't help you," he said, "we're not allowed to treat infantrymen. You need to leave."

I went out in the dark and lay on the ground dry-heaving for quite some time. Realizing I would soon go into shock, knowing I had to try something, I got up and went back inside.

"I'm gonna die and since you won't help me, you're going to have to watch me croak right here on the floor," I said, staring bleary-eyed at the orderly.

After 20 minutes of me dry heaving on the floor, he walked over.

"Okay, I'll help you," he said, "but it's gonna hurt!"

Like I cared!

He gave me some pills and watched as I swallowed them. He then helped me up and leaned me over a gurney.

"This *will* hurt," he announced.

I didn't look back, but it felt like he stabbed my left rear bun with a dull bayonet.

"Oooooooooooh!" I let out a painful moan.

He shoved me onto the gurney and I passed out after puking up the pills.

I woke up in the morning feeling better.

"Want some breakfast?" the orderly asked when he saw I was awake.

I was happy to see the change in his attitude. He took me next door to an Air Force mess hall where they had food the likes of which I hadn't seen in Vietnam.

37

SNEAKING HOME

The next day I was back on a chopper with my gear, headed to my platoon in the field. They had been in the rain a lot while I was gone. Someone sprayed the platoon with automatic weapons fire and Dale had been shot in the leg. He was a steel worker from North Carolina who had come over with us from Hawaii. He and Gary hung together and his great sense of humor was pretty entertaining. I'm sure Dale hoped it was one of those "I get to go home" wounds, but it wasn't, and he rejoined us after a few weeks.

I had not forgotten to make my nightly request for the men while I was gone. I'd only been back in the field a few days when some of us were called together. The captain announced that he had a seven-day "R&R" (Rest and Relaxation) leave to Hawaii to give one of us.

"I'll take it!" I offered.

A few days later, I was back on a chopper to our main firebase and headed for home.

Oh, I meant to say Hawaii.

At the firebase I picked up my orders, but had missed the paymaster and didn't have any cash. I hoped I could make things work out somehow. I caught a chopper ride to the next base where I was supposed to catch a standby flight to Hawaii. At the airport I ran into my platoon. I didn't know why they were there, and it really didn't matter, except they'd seen the paymaster and had money. Several guys pooled their cash and loaned me $1,000. They trusted me to come back.

It was a ten-hour flight to Hawaii but seemed short. Once there, I was briefed on what was expected of me.

"When you know where you're staying, call in and give us the location. Your return flight to Vietnam leaves in seven days at 0700 hours. Don't be late or miss your flight!"

I headed to a store where I bought some sandals, shorts, and a shirt. I changed clothes and went to the airport. I was in California six hours later.

It's hard to express what it was like being home and knowing at the same time that I had to go back. I still looked pale and gaunt from my recent bout with malaria.

It was early November and Mom fixed a Thanksgiving dinner. Pictures were taken with me getting food out of the refrigerator and of me sitting alone, knife and fork in hand, at a table completely covered with food. I had pictures of everything I could think of as proof of being home.

In the field we always talked about good food, torturing ourselves with the thoughts of what we missed the most: Mom's southern cooking on Sunday afternoons, pot roast with carrots, potatoes and gravy, fried peach pies, homemade ice cream, chocolate chip cookies, chili, big juicy hamburgers with fries, and a large glass filled with ice and Dr. Pepper.

Oink! Oink!

Before I'd left Vietnam, while I was borrowing cash from my buddies at the airport, there was talk circulating that our company would be heading into another situation like Tam Ky. It was worrisome dealing with those thoughts during my time at home. I expressed my concerns to Dad. I had changed and toughened considerably since the last time I had seen him, and he could tell. But Dad, in his dogged manner, had been continually putting his requests before God. He walked over to me, looked me in the eye, and stuck his finger in my chest.

"You'll be coming home."

I didn't ask him how he knew because he had always been honest and forthright with me.

A week spent in Vietnam went by very, very slowly, but that week at home flew by. All too soon I was on a plane headed back to Hawaii.

After landing, I thought it would be a good idea to check in early for my flight back to Hell. I knew it was supposed to leave at 0700, but I was thinking in civilian time now, and checked in at 4:00 p.m. for what I thought was my 7:00 p.m. flight. I walked over to the sarge at the reception center.

"I'm checking in early for my flight," I said.

"What's your name, soldier?" He was staring at me intently.

"Whitworth," I answered.

His stare intensified.

What was his problem?

He went ballistic.

"You didn't report where you were staying! We had no idea where you were!" he yelled.

Uh-oh! I'd goofed, but why was he so mad?

"Your flight left at 0700 this morning, soldier!"

Oh, gee whiz!

My thinking on civilian time had caused a little baby problem.

He took me to a room.

"Wait here!" he ordered.

He returned shortly with some paint and a brush.

"Paint the wood trim!" he ordered, and left.

He was gone about 20 minutes before coming back.

"There's a flight leaving at midnight, and you'd better be on it or your pay will be docked $458 for your flight back to Vietnam!"

Of course I would catch that flight! Heck, why would I want to pay my own way back to more gunfights and leech-infested jungles?

38

FRIENDLY FIRE

Before I knew it, I was back at LZ Bronco and out in the field. Two weeks later, when I got mail from home, it was a blast to show everyone the pictures of me sitting around the table with all that home cooking. I was definitely having a hard time getting used to those B-3 C-ration cookies with instant coffee again.

I had unintentionally kept the front door key to my folk's house in my pocket. It was in my fatigues, and I touched it often with the hope I would get to use it again someday. It was comforting to have it as a reminder of my dad's words to me about returning home.

I still hated nighttime patrols for all the obvious reasons: you could hardly see where you were going, it was easy to get lost, and things seemed to go wrong more often in the dark. By the time orders got passed down to me, they usually didn't include a description of where or why we were going. That night was no different, so as we left the firebase—I had no idea where we were headed. For some reason, we were staying in the trees that weren't too far from the outside perimeter. To my left, I could see the dark silhouette of the Quad-50 machine gun looming on the hill in the center of the firebase.

We were moving slowly through the bushes and trees when streaks of red tracer bullets started tearing up the foliage a short distance in front of us, and we heard the loud, unnerving cracks of trees being ripped apart by the rapid fire-power from the Quad-50. Limbs and chunks of wood were shredded as the wave of heavy machine-gun fire hammered through the trees, searching for its target. The gunner up on the hill must have spotted our movement with a starlight scope and thought we were the enemy. Fortunately, he was off target. The noise was tremendous and it was incredible to see what this gun could do up close! Needless to say, we felt some urgency to get it shut down quickly. The 50-caliber rounds would have sent us fleeing in horror if they had been any closer. Needless to say, though, we felt some urgency to get it shut down quickly. I could hear Dale screaming at someone over the radio with a great sense of urgency as he vehemently rattled off obscenities and bold verbiage, telling them to stop the incoming fire!

It took several minutes to get the gun shut down. Someone had obviously screwed up from the beginning of our operation. Either the right people weren't briefed that we were going to be out there, or we weren't supposed to be where the lieutenant had taken us.

Our platoon had been in on this kind of mistake before. That's when Frank proved once again how bold and insanely fearless he really was. We had been on a patrol in the jungle and needed to find the company perimeter that had been set up earlier in the day. We knew where the site was located and humped to it through the jungle-covered hills. When we finally arrived, we were ordered to find another location to spend the night because there wasn't enough room for all of us.

Feeling a little miffed, we took off, and within an hour or so came to a good spot on top of a hill about two "klicks" (2,000 meters) away. From our platoon's position, I could see trees and large rocks on the hill behind us and an area that resembled a saddle about a hundred yards out in front of us and down the hill. It was about 1600 hours once we got settled in, so we had an hour or two to clean and lubricate our weapons before nightfall.

Frank and I took apart the M60 machine gun and spread it

out on a poncho between us. Some of the other guys behind us were taking care of their equipment at the same time. As we sat there cleaning away, a barrage of bullets came ripping through our position.

I dove for the lowest spot I could see as bullets cracked by. The firing seemed like it was coming up at us from the saddle area below. Frank had seen something and instantly went wild; but instead of hitting the dirt, he jumped up and rapidly headed down the slope, furiously shaking his fist.

"You fatherless, incestuous, fornicators!" he screamed.

Wow!

Frank was so angry he wasn't paying any attention at all to those little bullets flying everywhere at 3,000 feet per second. Everyone jumped for some kind of cover and returned fire, but Frank stood shaking his fist and yelling out in the open.

"Get your heads out of your butts!"

Rex heard chatter coming over the radio that Third Platoon was making contact with the enemy. Fortunately, he figured out what was happening and started screaming into the mic.

"You S.O.B.s stop shooting at us!" he yelled. "You're shooting up Second Platoon you dimwits! Knock it off!"

Ric, Rex's buddy from Third Platoon, recognized his voice, realized something crazy was going on, and got them to cease firing.

At the time I wasn't sure why the bullets stopped and thought maybe those idiots down there had seen our tall madman running at them through the hail of bullets and understood his obscenities.

Frank came grumbling back, still so enraged he could hardly see straight.

We ended up with two wounded. When the mass of friendly bullets came ripping past us, Ace tried twisting out of the way and tore his knee out of place. I had always been envious of him because he was able to talk his way out of the field without much effort, but this time he was badly hurt and didn't return for a long time. The other guy was hit in the head by chunks of rock that broke off a boulder when bullets hit it. This little friendly-fire incident happened because word was never passed on that we had been sent away to find a different position for the night.

39

HOLIDAYS

We were doing the same old stuff—working from firebases, humping over the mountains and through the jungle, looking for Charlie and his supplies.

November 28, Thanksgiving Day, arrived here in the fields of Vietnam. We didn't have to go out on patrol, but were able to kick back and hope Charlie wouldn't interfere. This day wasn't special like at home when everyone's family gets together around the table to enjoy a great American meal, visiting, playing games, and getting caught up on the latest stories.

On Thanksgiving weekends at home, I'd go pheasant hunting with my buddies. I hadn't seen any pheasants here, but we did plenty of hunting.

Choppers flew in a dinner to us late in the afternoon, but it had been sitting around so long that the turkey was loaded. We didn't find this out until the middle of the night when we woke up with churning guts and repeatedly charged through the darkness to explosively dump the tainted meal.

I got out of the field for a short time because I still kept running a fever and was sent to LZ Bronco to recover. While I was there, the base was hit by incoming mortar and rocket attacks. Some were being fired from a big hill a couple of miles from the perimeter. While on nighttime bunker guard I could see 122mm rockets that Charlie was firing at us from there. Thankfully, they missed us.

President Johnson had stopped the bombing of the North a couple of months earlier and that was having a bad effect on our base camp. It seemed there was too much holding back. If

Johnson would only stop micro-managing things, the fight could be taken to the North with full air power and we could bomb their dams and other off-limits targets. Then we could finish this war and go home. Often things seem like they can be fixed simply, but this was a complicated war and would unfortunately take more than simple answers to end.

My fever left and it wasn't long before I was back out in the field and moving through the mountains again.

The days dragged on as we searched the area for Charlie. It seemed he didn't want to tangle with us directly, although we took his usual sniper fire, which kept us on our toes. During that time Lt. Dennis rotated out, and a few days later a replacement arrived, our third lieutenant since arriving in-country. One of the things that didn't make much sense was that an officer spent six months in the field while non-officers and draftees like me spent twelve. When a lieutenant or other officer finished his time with us, he was sent to the rear somewhere while we waited for someone new. Someone who not only didn't know us, but might not know very much about real combat either.

It became clear to me that the best place for an officer to make rank and advance his career was during a war. The Army hadn't been engaged like this for a long time, and now some of the career military folks were using the war to their advantage. I couldn't care less about career advancement. I wanted to see the war won and over, period. I didn't want to be put in unnecessary danger to advance someone's career or for other stupid reasons. But no one was asking me what I wanted.

When the new lieutenant came, it was obvious that he needed a little sharpening-up on his map-reading skills. For about his first month with us, we were lost in the mountains a lot. One time while we were playing Musical Mountains, climbing up and down for a full day, the green lieutenant couldn't figure out where we were. The guy walking point was tired of the lieutenant continually changing direction and was not happy to be wandering around. It was clear to him we were lost.

Finally, the lieutenant asked for high-explosive artillery rounds to be fired at a location near where he thought we were. After four or five rounds we heard one hit several miles from us. He then requested smoke rounds to be fired closer to our location, and we saw a round land near us. He confirmed by radio that the artillery was close. Since they knew where they had sent that round, they were able to give us our location on the map. At the end of the day, he finally knew where we were. Needless to say, we had little confidence in our new leader.

A few days later the whole company went on patrol. The new lieutenant had me set the machine gun up on a hill overlooking some smaller hills. The gun crew and I watched First Platoon move up one of the hills and disappear into the jungle. Soon after, the lieutenant came puffing up. He stepped over to me and pointed to the hill where First Platoon had gone.

"Put fire on that hill!" he ordered.

I'm sure I had a dumbfounded look on my face.

"Our men are in there!" I protested.

I could see he was getting angry and thought he might start in on me about my shallow gene pool. Instead, he again ordered me to start shooting into the hill.

"Yes, sir!" I replied crisply.

He turned around and started back down the hill. Our new "90-Day Wonder" didn't seem to be getting any smarter. I positioned myself behind the gun and sprayed a hundred rounds down into the jungle-covered hill—next to the one where our men had gone.

It had to be tough on him coming to a platoon where everyone knew more than he did about functioning in a combat zone, especially when he had a hard time listening. We weren't strangers to solving problems, and we worked hard to keep our new lieutenant from getting us getting caught with our pants down in Charlie's territory. A lot of us were short-timers and figured it would be better if we got along and did what we could to keep his ignorance from getting himself killed—and taking us out with him. He got better over time.

Over Christmas we were out in the jungle and had stayed in one place long enough that we dug foxholes around our perimeter and made our little poncho hooches to sleep under. Someone from home had sent one of the guys a tiny Christmas tree that he put in front of his hooch.

Merry Christmas!

We had been promised a turkey dinner and I was hoping for one that wasn't loaded. Our meal was delivered late in the day and it was another bad one. The turkey struck again. We sure had no lost love for the guys in the rear. It was not a silent night.

When we left our position and started to patrol the area, I realized that I had left a savings bond in my foxhole. Yeah, I finally bought some. A couple of days later, we came through that area again, and I took the opportunity to go look for my bond. I went to my foxhole, started digging around in the trash I had left behind, and found the bond. I also found a huge scorpion, about five inches long, with a two-inch-wide body that was a dark shiny green. What an exotic creature. It was beautiful, but I was glad it had waited until I'd vacated the foxhole before it took over.

We worked from numerous firebases during November and December. A few days after we had left a base in the mountains to patrol the jungle, we received word it had been overrun by NVA the night after we left. This was about the fourth time that had happened. I was trudging along behind Ralph, one of Third Squad's riflemen, while he walked point. I caught up with him when he stopped along the trail for a quick breather in the hot afternoon. As we stood there, he told me it felt like a big hand was covering us wherever we went.

I agreed with Ralph about us being protected. It seemed to be more than coincidence that most of the time we managed to make our way out of trouble.

40

HOPE'S STRENGTH

Hope is an interesting thing. When I had it, I could endure almost anything, but when it was gone, despair easily took hold, with dire consequences.

Some people may have never experienced the total and complete loss of hope and may have even wondered if such a horrible and frightening feeling existed. Others, unfortunately, discovered the reality that it happened in a flash when they realized the Grim Reaper was about to pay them a visit.

Some people tend to be natural optimists and think that bad stuff isn't going to happen to them. Positive thinking is a tool that lots of people believe will help them overcome anything. I was an optimist at heart and believed when facing a problem and had ten reasons why I couldn't succeed, I only needed one good reason why I could.

Having that outlook was good, but I needed more than the power of positive thinking. War and life's other problems had a way of devastating my outlook. It had been really hard for me to be optimistic or think positively during some of the situations I'd been through. There were some times that had been so devastating, that I thought I wasn't going to make it, and all hope vanished.

When we had been in-country for about three months, we'd headed up into the mountains, busting our rears, climbing from morning into the late afternoon. Hot and exhausted, we'd set up our perimeter on an open hilltop and began to get sniper fire coming in real close. Too close. I hunkered down, trying to stay out of sight, waiting, and hoping I was hidden.

Doubt and Fear paid me a visit, and thoughts of home and past events paraded through my mind. I had dealt with sniper fire before, but for some reason, that time it got to me, and I felt like I wasn't going to make it home alive.

As doubts settled in on me, my job seemed impossible. In no time, my hope completely faded away, and a terrible fear took hold of me. I had almost gone into a panic.

Lord, I need some help!

I was sure He knew how I felt because He had cried out, "My God, why have You forsaken me?"[16] when He hung on the cross. That must have been the most frightening place in the entire world.

What I had experienced was nothing in comparison, even though it felt very heavy to me. Eventually, those feelings faded, but the experience of sudden, overwhelming fear and my lack of hope for the future made a lasting impression.

I also thought I wasn't going to make it when we were fighting the battle near Tam Ky. On the fourth day, when we pushed hard into enemy fire and the track blew up in that huge explosion, for several minutes I had thought we were going to lose the battle. That shook me to the bone. All hope quickly drained away, and a miserable bleakness captured me. It was amazing that hope could vanish so quickly.

Those two experiences had shown me the emptiness of having no hope and how terrible that was. Even though they were terrifying, those lessons taught me that having hope was powerful and strong.

There's a scripture that says when you hang in during hard times, it builds character and produces hope.[17] Hope lifted my spirits and gave me a vision beyond the present. I needed that vision.

Hope was the beginning, a place where I could start looking ahead expectantly for a good outcome. Hope was seeing what I wanted in my mind, before I actually had it.

Hope was strengthened by knowledge. When information was available to work with, I better understood risk and failure. I wanted to never lack hope. It enhanced desire and motivated me to start looking for answers I didn't yet have. It helped me have patience while I moved toward accomplishing my goals. It strengthened me so I could put effort into risk and try to succeed. It was like wearing a pair of unique glasses to see past doubt.

Hope was a great foundation during stress and turmoil. It took effort to hold onto it, but when I did, it helped me live one day at a time, and some days, moment by moment. I didn't want to become like some, so wounded by life's trials, that I'd lose the desire for hope or a vision.

When Fear set in, Doubt's machine gun fired away, ripping off snappy strings of questions:

What if I took a sniper's bullet? What if I stepped on a land mine? What if I took the blast from an enemy's RPG?

I needed hope to find answers for those "what-ifs," and to fight off doubt.

I also needed hope to fight against those doubts that snuck into my mind when I was tired, pelting me with more negative questions.

Would I be killed if there was another gunfight like at Tam Ky, and this time Charlie didn't miss? Was I ready to die?

As much as I didn't like these questions, they were there. Facing the truth was necessary during those times, not dwelling on it excessively, but being real. I had no more guarantee that I would live than the next guy did, and I felt my mortality. Every day was full of deadly risk.

As soldiers, we helped each other have hope with truthful encouragement. We got strength from each other. We didn't necessarily talk about it, but we all shared the common hope that we would live through the war and make it home in one piece.

41

'55 CHEVY

We had been out in the field for a long stretch and needed a break. Our breather consisted of being sent to a firebase called LZ Cork high up in the mountains west of Duc Pho. This wasn't R&R. We still had to pull perimeter guard for the artillery guys and send out an occasional patrol. After a couple of weeks, we packed up our gear and headed out.

We started out of the perimeter and worked our way along a high ridgeline through thick jungle. It was slow going because we had to make our own trail along the ridge, mostly chopping our way through. By dusk we still hadn't found an area to set up our night perimeter. We pushed along because the ridge was narrow and the sides dropped off sharply. Soon it was dark.

Word was passed along that we were going to camp in place because we could no longer see where we were going. I stepped off the steep ridge, down to a tree a few feet away, sat down, and wrapped my legs around its trunk. Some other guys found trees down below me and we settled in for the night. I dug through my pack and found a can of apricots and a hot can of Coke. We could buy two cans of soda or two beers a week if a chopper brought them out with supplies. I tried to save a Coke as long as I could, because it was a great bartering tool. Well, dinner tonight wasn't going to be much.

The tree kept me from sliding down the ridge into the darkness, and it actually didn't take much to fall asleep, even on a 45-degree angle. I woke up at about 0200 hours, sick to my stomach and started barfing down the ridge. The guys below me didn't think too highly of my contribution and began changing my name.

In the morning, we continued moving across the ridge and down toward the foothills that separated us from the rice paddies and villages where we were headed. About midmorning we stopped for a break.

Steve and I were kicking back and I used the time to write home to Beth. He was interested in who I was writing and asked about her.

"She's a gorgeous blonde with brains, and that's all you need to know," I said.

I couldn't help myself though, and dug a plastic-covered picture of her out of my pack and let him take a look.

"Whoa," he said, "no woman that good-looking should be waiting for a chump like you."

Steve didn't give up.

"I think I'll drop her a line myself."

He started writing her a letter, saying some real smooth sweet stuff that I had never even thought of.

"If I was an artist I couldn't paint my feelings for you. If I was a poet I couldn't put it in verse."

Steve wrote like a cotton-pickin' Casanova and went on like that for a couple of pages. He even had the words spelled right, something Beth wasn't used to seeing in my letters. When Casanova was done with his love letter, he handed it to me and I saw he signed it with a flourish.

"All my love, Arthur Godfrey."

What a guy! Steve was real smooth with words; maybe he would help me write a nice letter home to get some cookies sent our way. I stuck his letter in the envelope with mine, sealed and addressed it, then wrote "Free" where the stamp was to go. I stuffed it in my pocket to mail at my earliest opportunity.

It took us several days to work our way down to the foothills. We were crossing a creek and started goofing around, throwing small boulders in the water and splashing each other. I was carrying the machine gun and was having a hard time dodging some of the boulders. One of them landed on my foot. By the time we got down to the flatland, my foot was swollen and I was barely able to hobble.

A chopper landed with some supplies, and two new fellas got off to join the company. I had noticed them a couple of weeks earlier when I went to the doc about headaches I had been having. One of them had a scarf around his neck and was wearing a holstered .45 pistol. He was practicing a quick-draw and doing his best to be macho. It had been worrisome watching him try to play the part. I thought to myself that these guys had no idea what they were in for.

I got on the chopper and it headed for base. When we arrived, I found a place where I could bunk, then dropped my letter in the mail and limped toward the chow hall.

I went to see the doc in the morning. My foot was still swollen and painful. They wrapped it up, put me on crutches, and told me to keep off it a few days and then come back to have it checked again. I hobbled around on the crutches and mainly tried to stay out of trouble by keeping to myself and being hard to find. I didn't want to be assigned bunker duty or put way out on some hill on an all-night listening post that was hit every night by Charlie.

Sometimes in the evening the firebase would show a movie on a big wooden structure that was painted white. This was a real treat that grunts like me seldom got. The screen was set in about 150 yards from the barbed-wire perimeter and bunker line.

I hobbled across a field between the large movie screen and the bunker line, climbed up some stairs made from wooden ammo boxes to the benches, picked a spot, and sat down. As I waited for it to get dark enough for the movie to start, other soldiers filled the benches next to me. From where I sat I could see most of the open area behind the screen and about 2,000 yards past the perimeter to a tree line on the other side of the rice paddies. I was looking out at the tree line and saw some flashes.

Doop! Doop! Doop! Doop! Doop!

I heard the sounds a mortar makes as it's fired.

Doop! Doop! Doop! Doop!

Nine Soviet 82mm mortars were headed our way. Once the VC fired off their rounds they usually grabbed up the four-foot-long mortar tube and took off as quickly as they could. If they waited around, they would be ripped to pieces by the .50 caliber rounds from the Quad-50 behind us.

The benches emptied in a flash and everybody started running for the bunkers. I didn't have any good choices. I could try to get down the stairs and make a mad stumble for the bunkers, or stay put. There were only seconds left until the mortars hit.

I wasn't the only one not under cover. As I looked out on the field in front of me, I saw a lone soldier running as fast as his short legs would carry him. His right arm was through the armhole of his flack-jacket and he had his M16 in that hand. He was reaching back unsuccessfully trying to get his left arm through the other armhole as he headed toward the bunker line along the perimeter's edge. He was right in front of me, about 60 yards out.

As I watched him run, all nine mortars landed right where he was. I couldn't see him anymore because of the huge cloud of dust and dirt blown up into the air. Some of the shrapnel hit the wood screen to my right. I waited a minute or two as the dust settled, thinking that there wouldn't be much left of him. I still had the terrible images of the guys who had been killed at Tam Ky in my head, and was in no hurry to see another mangled body.

The first time I had experienced anything that looked like a miracle, I was 16 and driving a '55 Chevy I had recently bought from a buddy's dad. It was a two-door sedan painted blue and white. I loved that car and usually drove it too fast. That particular day wasn't any different. I was on the highway, doing 80 in the right lane, and having a great time listening to the radio as Elvis sang, "You ain't nothin' but a hound dog." I wasn't paying much attention to the road.

I looked up and saw a blue '49 Pontiac with four old men in it, going about 25 right in front of me. I slammed on the brakes and lost control of the Chevy as it began to spin in circles. We didn't wear seat belts in those days and my car didn't have them anyway. My body was being thrown all around the front seat while I held onto the steering wheel with one hand. When the car straightened out I looked up and saw a large telephone pole three feet in front of the hood. Still moving at high speed, I figured I was about to die.

I simply said, "Jesus! Help!"

The Chevy instantly moved to the left and headed back to the highway. My right leg didn't stop shaking for the next 20 miles.

I thought I heard moaning coming from the vicinity where the mortars landed.

No way! He's still alive?

I stood up and hobbled down the stairs and out to where he was lying in a crumpled mess. He had dirt all over him and was quietly moaning. I was amazed.

"Where are you hurt?" I asked him.

He moved his hand and I could see where a quarter-size piece of shrapnel had gone through the palm of his left hand. It wasn't bleeding badly and as I looked him over more closely I couldn't see any major wounds.

No one was coming out of the bunker line to help, so I bent down and lifted him up, pulling his arm over my shoulder. I struggled along, half dragging him the 90 yards to the closest bunker. He wasn't saying a word. There was no telling what else was wrong with him.

I got him inside and laid him on a bunk in the corner. I told the guys in the bunker what had happened, but they were so shook up about the mortar attack that they didn't know what to do. I figured the worst was over and that they would calm down and radio for a medic, so I left.

I've always wondered who that guy was and how he did after I left. I'm not saying it was a miracle that he hadn't been killed instantly—but I'll bet he thinks it was.

The next day I ran into Frank. I was surprised to see him.

"Frank, what's up? How come you're not out in the field with the rest of the guys?"

Then I noticed there was fresh blood on his clothes.

"What happened?" I asked.

"I'm okay," he answered. "This is from those two new guys who came out when you left. I was coming in for the doc to check the sores on my feet when the chopper I was on was sent back to pick up their bodies."

"Bodies?" I asked. "What happened?"

"After you left on the supply chopper, the company moved to a nearby village where a firefight broke out with Charlie. During the exchange, those two guys revealed themselves while returning fire and both were killed."

It was good to see Frank, but it was a sad deal. Those poor guys only lasted a few days in the field and never had a chance to learn that firefights were dangerous and for-real, not like some John Wayne movie.

I milked all the time I could out of my crushed foot but I was only allowed a short time in the rear. What the heck. I had slept all night long for a few nights and gotten three hot meals a day. During one meal the VC had dropped in a few mortars so Frank and I had the whole chow hall to ourselves again. It was every bit as good as the last time. Everyone here too, cooks and all, vacated the building in a flash when they heard the cry of "incoming!"

The enemy was getting plenty of supplies now that the bombing of North Vietnam had stopped, and these guys were starting to get mortared and rocketed more often. So, I didn't complain too much when I was informed they were sending me back out to the field on the next available chopper.

42

THE WILDEST RIDE

I was promoted to E5. Now I would be paid $300 a month. I had been sending most of my money home in hopes I would be rich (ha! ha!) when I got back. There sure wasn't much to spend it on here. By this time, I was getting to be a short-timer and a wee bit jumpy. We were in the mountains looking for Charlie and I had written home to Mom.

"Send goodies. They're feeding us dog food here."

After humping up and down the hills, we made it to a firebase in the mountains. It took awhile to get settled into a position on the perimeter. We were pretty far back in the jungle. After we had the machine gun's field of fire laid out and Claymores set up, we kicked back. Out in front of us someone had called in an air strike. It was pretty far off and I couldn't tell what the target was or if the bombs were hitting it. At least we had a show to entertain us for a while. During this time we started getting sniper fire, but the guy was a lousy shot and nobody bothered to dive for cover. The jungle was so dense we couldn't tell where to return fire anyway.

We actually got to rest up a couple of weeks at this location. The perimeter was probed often and there were a few hot spots. I had heard that Charlie made it into one guy's position and dragged him down the hill in the dark. The soldier managed to hang onto a hand grenade and was able to beat the gooks off with it and get away. Of course, incidents like that helped keep me awake on guard.

A supply chopper dropped off some mail and I got a box

of candy from Davis, my rabbit-hunting/water-skiing buddy at home. It was something I wouldn't forget. It was easy for your buddies back in the world to forget about you or never even wonder what was happening with you. The draft just sucked you off the street and you were gone.

Being a grunt in the field wasn't conducive to pulling out a runny pen to write on soaking-wet paper in order to keep pen pals informed about your tropical military vacation and all the hot resorts where you had been staying. You weren't sharing with them the delicious taste of food and mixed drinks you were enjoying; the sweet B3 cookies and great instant iodine coffee you drank under your poncho while it was raining cats and dogs and you soaked up the atmosphere.

After a while we were informed we would be heading off the firebase, so we got our gear ready. We packed away C-rations and the same old stuff; plenty of ammo, trip flares, grenades, mines, and rockets. Then off the hill and down into the small valleys we went, crossing creeks, and working our way through the jungle.

A lot of us were short-timers so we were very careful about not getting lax and giving Charlie a chance to catch us with our pants down. We humped over mountains and through the jungle for days looking for him. When we set up our nighttime perimeters, the forward observer for artillery called in 105 spotter rounds. It helped me sleep a little better knowing we had this kind of fire support. Maybe I had developed a better appreciation for it now that I was getting closer to going home.

We were in the field for a long time doing our search and destroy stuff. Finally, we reached the edge of the mountains and climbed up a large hill that overlooked the flat country and rice paddies below. There was a firebase at the top of the hill with 105mm artillery. We were sent there to pull perimeter guard while new replacements were being sent to take our place in the field. It felt unbelievable, but we were going to be sent to the rear in a few days to begin the process of going home.

Those of us who were leaving were a large part of Second Platoon and were trusted for our experience. TC and some of the other guys who had joined us a few months back would be the old-timers now because new soldiers would be taking our places. This was cause for apprehension, because new guys had a lot to learn, pronto! Until they got acclimated, they were a danger to themselves and others.

One of the guys who wasn't leaving yet stopped by my position with a question. I had become somewhat acquainted with him in the time he was with us.

"Bob," he asked, "Is there any way to stop being afraid?"

It wasn't exactly an easy question. I had an answer, but I didn't think he would like it, and for good reason.

Fear had been my almost constant companion. It had worn me out. It was the helper I hated. It made me look more closely at my situations. It had made me look closer at myself and sometimes I didn't like what I saw. Even though I didn't want to, I'd found that I always had to confront fear.

"I don't know," I replied, "I do know one thing though, don't give in to it."

One of the most memorable times I had faced fear was during the summer I worked at a potato-processing plant to earn money for my first car. During that time I became acquainted with Roy-Dean. Roy was nine or ten years older than I was and loved hot-rod cars as much as I did. He had a 1927 Chrysler coupe, and under the hood was stuffed a 409 cubic-inch Chevy engine with two 4-barrel carburetors. It also had street slicks mounted on the rear mag-rims and a beefed-up B&M hydro transmission. There was only a driver's seat. The passenger sat on a wooden pop-bottle box on the metal floorboard. It was a shell of a car with no interior or seat belts.

I had been bugging Roy for some time to give me a ride. One Friday evening I saw him drive into the local hangout. He motioned to me.

"Jump in, Bob. We'll drag Main."

That usually meant we would drive a quarter-mile down Main Street through town, stop at all the stop signs, and wave at the girls and all our friends as we drove by. I opened the door and sat down on the short hard box. We pulled out and headed down Main Street. That's when I smelled alcohol on Roy.

When we rumbled up to the first of the four stop signs, I could see there were a lot of people on Main Street and plenty of traffic around. It had been very hot that day and people were coming out to shop as it cooled off.

After pausing a few seconds at the stop sign next to the JC Penney store, Roy slammed the big aluminum foot-shaped gas pedal to the floor, and smoke started boiling from the rear tires as they began to spin. My head was slammed back, banging against the rear window, and my body was pinned against the back of the car as we roared toward the next stop sign. I thought Roy would start putting on the brakes at any second, but he didn't. He just kept the pedal to the metal and we flew right through the next stop sign, picking up speed as the transmission slammed into the next gear.

The hot-rod was going like a bat out of hell as we hurtled through crosswalks and intersections where cars were pulling out. I couldn't make a sound, let alone get a word out. I was terrified that we would run over someone or crash into a car full of people crossing an intersection. The stores, people, sidewalks, parking meters, stop signs, and telephone poles all turned into a blur as we raced the entire length of Main Street, never stopping. At about 130 miles an hour, Roy let off the gas pedal and started applying the brakes, ending the most fearful, stupid, and hazardous ride I'd ever had in my life.

At that time, I'd had no idea of what my future would hold, but there had been a ride coming my way that had no seat belts or brakes, and the collision was meant to be. It would turn out to be the wildest ride of my life. The dab of fear I'd felt on

Main Street that warm Friday evening wasn't even on the chart compared to what I had come to know and learned to deal with in Vietnam.

From the hill, we watched as artillery pounded an enemy position in the valley below. Then an air strike was sent to finish it off. It sure felt good, knowing we wouldn't have to go down there and clean up after it was over.

Some endeavors in life were frightening for me to even try—like jumping off a high diving board, scuba diving, flying, skydiving, or whatever. As I gained knowledge about those endeavors, my fears dissipated. But in a combat situation, I couldn't get enough information about what might be going down. It was really scary to think that I could get my body parts blown off or get killed.

By facing my fears and forcing myself to acknowledge them, I put my mind to work on ways of overcoming them. I had to determine what would be the worst that could happen, and work back from there.

"Prepare for the worst and hope for the best."

Once I decided to do that, I looked for a balance I could live with. This was hard to do, but it helped me find a way through fear. I learned to accept that the worst might happen, and if it did, I could pray with faith asking Jesus to be with me.

The Bible says, "Fear not for I am with you."[18]

Those words helped me.

The air strike was over and we spent some time gathering gear and saying our goodbyes. Then we boarded the Hueys for our last chopper ride out of the field. We arrived at LZ Bronco and began processing out. The duffle bags we had brought with us from Hawaii had been left behind a long year ago when we first left Bronco. During the time we were in the field, the storage tent, with our stuff in it, was destroyed.

I turned in my gear, putting a few things from my rucksack into a small satchel. I wasn't going to miss the hardware I had been carrying. I was given clean jungle fatigues with sergeant's stripes on the shirt for the first time. I put the house key into my clean pocket.

We got our orders and were flown south to Cam Rahn Bay where we boarded a World Airways jet.

We were on our way home.

Alive.

43

BACK TO THE WORLD

It was one of the happiest days of my life—April 14, 1969. My tour had ended. I was in Vietnam one day and back in the U.S. the next. Taking off from Cam Rahn Bay, we landed at Fort Lewis where I was given a new Class-A uniform, my pay, and an airplane ticket home. My time in the U.S. military had consisted of nearly a year in training and a full 12 months in Vietnam. I was discharged from active duty and three days later was back in California.

Beth and my family were thrilled to see me come home in one piece! Dad, being the man that he was, somehow grasped how I felt about what I had been through. I knew that whenever I was ready to talk, he would be there to listen. He continued to be the strong, steadfast man he always had been. It was good knowing he was near. He wasn't just my father, he was my friend, too.

I thought the war was over for me, but coming back to the world wasn't what I thought it would be. There were no welcoming parties or parades. No "Welcome home, Soldier. Thank you for serving our country." Instead, many at home were filled with disrespect and disdain toward the men who were fighting to give others the same hope of freedom that they enjoyed.

This didn't make any sense to me. It felt strange and was very frustrating to watch the news and see our country in turmoil about the war. The news media continually hammered away against the war with no consideration for the soldiers who fought and served. Despite their opinion of the situation in Vietnam, it just wasn't right for them to turn their backs on those of us who had paid and would continue to pay a price for answering the call of our country.

Before I'd left, I was like everyone else in the U.S. who really couldn't appreciate how rich our country was. We didn't realize how much was available to us that others around the world didn't have—benefits and opportunities that we took for granted. But now, I had a very high appreciation for what it meant to live in the United States.

Even the simple pleasures I had done without took on new meaning. I was grateful for the things most people never even think about—like sleeping under a roof out of the rain and bad weather. I would have been happy to sleep safely on the dry dirt under my father's house.

Having clean clothes, dry feet, taking a shower every night, and eating whatever and whenever I wanted were just a few of the things that made being home again almost unbelievable. It felt too good to be true.

I didn't realize it at the time, but the knowledge I had acquired during my tour of duty had changed my perspective about life. Before I went to Vietnam, I was just as naïve as everyone at home seemed to be about danger. We all took it for granted that nothing could go wrong, but now my definition of "normal" had changed. Life was not carefree anymore.

It was now normal for me to always be vigilant. It was normal for me to avoid being in a crowd. It was normal for me to sit facing windows or doors so I could see what was coming. At night in the dark, I still felt I might not be safe.

I could barely tolerate it when I saw people who were experiencing sad or painful feelings and emotions. Didn't they know they should just suck it up and get on with life? Since my feelings had been seared by my experiences, I would turn anything close to tender feelings into a joke and laugh it off so I wouldn't have to deal with it.

Things like this showed Beth just how much I had changed. Although I "came home," she said I was still a soldier with a hard-core attitude and she was forced to realize that it wasn't going away any time soon. I had no idea that I was missing out on a great part of the richness of life.

I made an effort to fit into civilian life again. Beth and I got married on May 20, a month after I came home. I stayed busy getting reacquainted with old friends and trying to get back to work. It was awkward, however, when someone asked, "What have you been up to?"

What answer did I have for that simple question? I hadn't been to any movies lately, no bird hunting or fishing trips to talk about, no drag races or fast-car stories. There were a few little war stories I could tell, but the reality of war was something I couldn't explain.

My faith in Jesus was still as important to me as ever. The Bible was full of inspiration that I dug out through reading and studying as I struggled with the memories of war, while at the same time working to put our lives on the right track. In I Corinthians it says that we have three things abiding with us: faith, hope and love.[19] I was building faith, had my hope renewed, but I felt more than a little short on love. I was going to need some powerful help with that one.

Beth knew how much I trusted God and the effort I made not to give in to my impulses. To her credit, she loved and prayed for me through my troubles with the mental and physical residue and sleepless nights. She rescued me many times with her prayers, love, and faithfulness.

Though the carefree, young soldier she had said goodbye to earlier did not resemble the troubled man she now married, she continued to love and care for me, patiently waiting for the man she had known to show through my hardened shell. She had faith and believed that God would continue to guide and be with us.

She did have some concerns though. I had many triggers and would startle easily. And because of the misrepresentation of the media about Vietnam vets, until she got better acquainted with the "new and improved" me, she didn't know for sure whether I would lose control and react unfavorably to some of the situations I encountered.

Many people were unsure about us veterans. The truth was, we were disciplined soldiers returning from war. We knew how to obey orders. We were trained to exercise patience under dangerous circumstances. We weren't loose cannons, going around destroying everything in our lives. We had left as boys, but came home as men, troubled by war and rejected by our country.

I went into the California State Office of Unemployment looking for a job. During my interview, the woman asked what kind I work I did in the Army. As soon I said I was an infantry soldier and had operated machine guns and small arms in Vietnam, I was treated with disdain and received little help. This only compounded the rejection I felt. Regardless of these put-downs, I managed to keep my cool.

I finally found a job on my own. However, I didn't realize that I had been conditioned to be a soldier for years to come. It took little to trigger me back to being in what I thought was a deadly situation. My reactions were as much a part of me as breathing. Some of my buddies and the guys at work got great pleasure from surprising me or making loud noises that would have me instantly hitting the floor. I couldn't control this impulse. I have to admit that it must have looked quite funny, watching me drop down looking for cover. I'm sure they had no idea what effect their pranks really had on me.

After a while, Beth and I signed up for several courses at our local junior college to enhance our academic skills. During one of the classes, our elderly female instructor launched into an angry tirade about how cruel our U.S. forces behaved in Vietnam and began to praise the NVA soldiers and VC.

I wondered for a few seconds if we had mistakenly signed up for a course in Communism 101. Anger boiled inside me as she desecrated the commitment our soldiers made and the high price paid in toil, pain, and death. I instantly knew I had two choices. I stood up and leaned forward, grasping the table in front of me with both hands. I could jump over the table and release my anger on her, proving we were what she said, or take the hardest course of action and do what I knew was right.[20]

Beth sat beside me holding her breath, waiting to see what I was going to do. Against my desire, I turned and walked out of the room.

Even though it was brutal, the simplicity of life in Vietnam had been clear. While I was there, my main objective was to stay alive. I hadn't had the privilege of thinking about or dealing with the tragedies that were taking place. My mind hid them away somewhere deep inside as I continued moving, alert and on guard.

Now that I was home, whether I wanted to or not, I relived events over and over. In some ways life became agonizing. I wanted something to dull that pain. In an effort to deal with the anguish inside of me I could easily have cartwheeled off into drugs or alcohol along with any other pleasure I could find.

I vividly remember sitting in my car late one night at my dad's gas station contemplating how to find relief from my pounding memories.

Why shouldn't I start drinking; just head over to the bar and tie a good one on.

As badly as I wanted to accept the temporary relief calling my name, I decided to stick with what I knew and hang in for the long haul.

I knew that I had experienced things that were hard to believe. How did hand grenades not explode, bullets and shrapnel continually miss, sickness not kill, snakes not strike, and stupidity not do us in? Some might say living through the dangers we faced was coincidence or luck. I couldn't say that. I knew God had been there, invisibly helping, even when death was present. Death has a sting all its own and it affects all who it touches.

Some of what happened during my tour I still have no words for, only pictures in my mind that I don't want to see. Most combat veterans have pictures like that. Getting to the place where you are willing to look at and work through them takes time and some good help. It's never too late to get that help.

I continued to go to God for hope and help, and was determined to work my way through the problems and challenges I knew were ahead. I brought my struggles to Him: the disturbing concerns I had, the misperceptions I faced, and the anger I held against those who unjustly accused those of us who had served our country faithfully.

At night, when I couldn't face reliving the troubles that played on the movie screen of my dreams, my mind turned to Him. I knew that I had to wait patiently for His strength—and it came. I treasured the scriptures, "The just shall live by faith, but He takes no pleasure in him who turns back," and "Cast all your cares upon Me."[21] Even with all I knew, and my prayers, I still really struggled.

There were times when I seemed to be robbed of all that was good. My worst reasoning told me that staying alive just to live in an empty wilderness of void and pain, wasn't worthwhile. When I was weakened by those thoughts, I felt like death was a valid alternative. That was a lie that was easy to believe. It was a dangerous place to be.

What helped me during those times was being able to trust the Bible. The meaning I found there about life kept me going. It told me to forgive,[22] and to do what was right. This was the opposite of what was natural in any man, but I knew it was a place of strength. It was surely better than the empty wasteland where my own reasoning led.

We have no way of knowing under what circumstances we might become a part of death, or be surrounded by troubles that can affect us for years. It happened to me and it can happen to anyone.

God's Word gives life and is a rock to stand on when everything else has been washed away. I wasn't in the Army anymore, but still had a Commander—one I trusted. One who instead of avoiding danger, faced it head-on. When all was said and done, He had secured the prize of eternal life for all who trust in Him. I had learned that Jesus wouldn't necessarily take me out of trouble, but would be with me through it, teaching me how to trust Him. His Word gave me power beyond myself to move on.

John 16:33 says, "These things I have spoken to you, that in Me you may have peace. In the world you will have tribulation; but be of good cheer, I have overcome the world." I stood on the truth I had read and learned, and it brought me hope for my future and faith that things would work out—not necessarily my way, but the right way.[23] That knowledge gave me a reason to keep going and courage not to quit. That hope helped me move forward in life and, even if I failed, I would fail forward.

At first glance many are not interested in knowing Jesus and think there is no substance to the Bible. Some call this a crutch or whatever… but there comes a time when it's clear we need help.

Give Jesus a chance. Come to Him privately. Ask Him to forgive your sins; as few or many as there are.[24] Begin the journey, join His family, and develop a real relationship with Him.[25]

I have never regretted my decision to trust God, even when things happened that I didn't understand. I was pointed in this direction early on, but it still had to stand the hard tests of life. My hope's foundation is the One who cares for my soul, Who died for my sins, and proved Himself trustworthy. Jesus has given me hope and answers to life's questions. He is my friend, my source of inspiration, and my anchor in life's storms.[26]

REFERENCES

All Scripture References are from the New King James Version unless otherwise noted.

[1] Do not be afraid of sudden terror, nor of trouble from the wicked when it comes; For the LORD will be your confidence, and will keep your foot from being caught.

Proverbs 3:25, 26

———

[2] No place so sacred from such fops is barr'd, nor is Paul's Church more safe than Paul's Church-yard: Nay, fly to altars; there they'll talk you dead; for fools rush in where angels fear to tread.

An Essay on Criticism by Alexander Pope – 1709

———

[3] A thousand may fall at your side, and ten thousand at your right hand; but it shall not come near you.

Psalm 91:7

———

[4] Love suffers long and is kind; love does not envy; love does not parade itself, is not puffed up; does not behave rudely, does not seek its own, is not provoked, thinks no evil; does not rejoice in iniquity, but rejoices in the truth; bears all things, believes all things, hopes all things, endures all things. Love never fails.

I Corinthians 13:4-8a

———

[5] Where there is no vision, the people perish: but he that keepeth the law, happy is he.

Proverbs 29:18 (King James Version)

⁶ Now faith is the substance of things hoped for, the evidence of things not seen.

Hebrews 11:1

"Now the just shall live by faith; But if anyone draws back, My soul has no pleasure in him."

Hebrews 10:38

For we walk by faith, not by sight. *2 Corinthians 5:7*

---

⁷ But Jesus kept silent. And the high priest answered and said to Him, "I put You under oath by the living God: Tell us if You are the Christ, the Son of God!" Jesus said to him, *"It is as you said."*

Matthew 26:63, 64

And truly Jesus did many other signs in the presence of His disciples, which are not written in this book; but these are written that you may believe that Jesus is the Christ, the Son of God, and that believing you may have life in His name.

John 20:30, 31

---

⁸ How much better to get wisdom than gold! And to get understanding is to be chosen rather than silver.

Proverbs 16:16

---

⁹ But certainly God has heard me; He has attended to the voice of my prayer. Blessed be God, who has not turned away my prayer, nor His mercy from me!

Psalm 66:19, 20

^{10} Be anxious for nothing, but in everything by prayer and supplication, with thanksgiving, let your requests be made known to God.

Philippians 4:6

---

^{11} For we do not have a High Priest who cannot sympathize with our weaknesses, but was in all points tempted as we are, yet without sin.

Hebrews 4:15

---

^{12} Are there crosses too heavy to carry, and burdens too heavy to bear, are there heartaches and tears and anguish and no one who seems to care? Are there shadows of deep disappointment and trusts that have proven untrue; has the darkness of night settled round you, has your hope and your faith wavered too? Has the storm overshadowed your sunshine, and life lost attraction for you, have the dreams that you cherished been broken, is your soul filled with bitterness too? Standing somewhere in the shadows you'll find Jesus, He's the Friend who always cares and understands. Standing somewhere in the shadows you will find Him and you'll know Him by the nail-prints in His hands.

"Standing Somewhere in the Shadows"
by E. J. Rollings

---

^{13} Confess your trespasses to one another, and pray for one another, that you may be healed. The effective, fervent prayer of a righteous man avails much.

James 5:16

¹⁴ My brethren, count it all joy when you fall into various trials, knowing that the testing of your faith produces patience. But let patience have its perfect work, that you may be perfect and complete, lacking nothing.

James 1:2-4

---

¹⁵ Blessed is the man who trusts in the LORD, and whose hope is the LORD.

Jeremiah 17:7

---

¹⁶ And about the ninth hour Jesus cried out with a loud voice, saying, *"Eli, Eli, lama sabachthani?"* that is, *"My God, My God, why have You forsaken Me?"*

Matthew 27:46

---

¹⁷ And not only that, but we also glory in tribulations, knowing that tribulation produces perseverance; and perseverance, character; and character, hope. Now hope does not disappoint, because the love of God has been poured out in our hearts by the Holy Spirit who was given to us.

Romans 5:3-5

---

¹⁸ Fear not, for I am with you; Be not dismayed, for I am your God. I will strengthen you, Yes, I will help you, I will uphold you with My righteous right hand.

Isaiah 41:10

---

¹⁹ And now abide faith, hope, love, these three; but the greatest of these is love.

I Corinthians 13:13

---

[20] A soft answer turns away wrath, but a harsh word stirs up anger.

Proverbs 15:1

A quick-tempered man acts foolishly, and a man of wicked intentions is hated.

Proverbs 14:17

So then, my beloved brethren, let every man be swift to hear, slow to speak, slow to wrath; for the wrath of man does not produce the righteousness of God.

James 1:19, 20

---

[21] "Now the just shall live by faith; but if anyone draws back, My soul has no pleasure in him."

Hebrews 10:38

Therefore humble yourselves under the mighty hand of God, that He may exalt you in due time, casting all your care upon Him, for He cares for you.

I Peter 5:6

---

[22] *"And forgive us our sins, for we also forgive everyone who is indebted to us. And do not lead us into temptation, but deliver us from the evil one."*

Luke 11:4

Then Peter came to Him and said, "Lord, how often shall my brother sin against me, and I forgive him? Up to seven times?" Jesus said to him, *"I do not say to you, up to seven times, but up to seventy times seven."*

Matthew 18:21, 22

²³ And we know that all things work together for good to those who love God, to those who are the called according to His purpose.

Romans 8:28

---

²⁴ Even the righteousness of God, through faith in Jesus Christ, to all and on all who believe. For there is no difference; for all have sinned and fall short of the glory of God, being justified freely by His grace through the redemption that is in Christ Jesus.

Romans 3:22-24

"For God so loved the world that He gave His only begotten Son, that whoever believes in Him should not perish but have everlasting life. For God did not send His Son into the world to condemn the world, but that the world through Him might be saved."

John 3:16, 17

For when we were still without strength, in due time Christ died for the ungodly. For scarcely for a righteous man will one die; yet perhaps for a good man someone would even dare to die. But God demonstrates His own love toward us, in that while we were still sinners, Christ died for us.

Romans 5:6-8

If we confess our sins, He is faithful and just to forgive us our sins and to cleanse us from all unrighteousness.

I John 1:9

For by grace you have been saved through faith, and that not of yourselves; it is the gift of God, not of works, lest anyone should boast.

Ephesians 2:8, 9

[25] *"Come to Me, all you who labor and are heavy laden, and I will give you rest. Take My yoke upon you and learn from Me, for I am gentle and lowly in heart, and you will find rest for your souls. For My yoke is easy and My burden is light."*

Matthew 11:28-30

"As the Father loved Me, I also have loved you; abide in My love. If you keep My commandments, you will abide in My love, just as I have kept My Father's commandments and abide in His love. These things I have spoken to you, that My joy may remain in you, and that your joy may be full."

John 15:9-11

[26] This hope we have as an anchor of the soul, both sure and steadfast, and which enters the Presence behind the veil, where the forerunner has entered for us, even Jesus, having become High Priest forever according to the order of Melchizedek.

Hebrews 6:19, 20

For I am persuaded that neither death nor life, nor angels nor principalities nor powers, nor things present nor things to come, nor height nor depth, nor any other created thing, shall be able to separate us from the love of God which is in Christ Jesus our Lord.

Romans 8:38, 39

GLOSSARY OF TERMS

AK47 – A lightweight Soviet or Chinese 7.62 assault rifle.

AMBUSH – Lying in wait to shoot or detonate explosive devices against the opposing side. Ambushes were conducted by both American and Vietnamese forces. It was no fun to be on one or caught in one.

AMMO – Ammunition.

APC – Armored Personnel Carrier. Also called a "track," an APC usually had two .30 caliber and one .50 caliber machine gun mounted on it. Great to work with, but when it broke down, it seemed like every enemy sniper in the area would shoot at it—and us—while we tried to get it mobile again.

ARVN – Army of the Republic of Viet Nam. South Vietnamese soldier.

AUTOMATIC WEAPONS – Machine guns, AK47s, M16s, M60s, or M2s (.50 caliber); to name a few.

AWOL – Absent without official leave.

BOOBY TRAP – A concealed explosive device that would detonate when touched.

BOONIES – The countryside; isolated rural/wilderness locations.

BOUNCING BETTY MINE – A nightmarish 9-pound, 5" x 4" diameter explosive. When tripped, it bounced three to five feet in the air before it exploded. Deadly out to 22 yards.

BRASS – Officers, upper echelon.

BRONZE STAR – Decoration awarded by the United States of America for heroic or meritorious achievement or service. "V" device fastened to ribbon, awarded with medal for valor.

BUNKER – Protective shelter. (American) Reinforced with timber and steel and covered with sandbags or ammunition boxes filled with soil. (Enemy) Mound of dirt over a hole that was reinforced from below with logs and packed earth and often covering the entrance to a cave or maze of tunnels.

C-4 – Plastic explosive in Claymore mines.

CACHE – A hiding place for safekeeping and storage of provisions, valuables or weapons.

CHARLIE – Slang for the VC (Viet Cong) or NVA (North Vietnamese Army).

CHICOM GRENADE – A Chinese-Communist hand grenade.

CHINOOK – A large twin-rotor transport or cargo helicopter.

CHOP-CHOP – Food.

CHOPPER – Helicopter. Usually had a four-man crew with a .30 caliber machine gun mounted next to each side door. Used to supply and transport grunts to and from locations, rescue them, and save them hundreds of miles of walking. Grunts loved them.

CICADA – Large insect whose male makes a shrill sound.

CLAYMORE – A mine weighing 3.5 pounds, filled with C-4 explosive and ball bearings. Deadly to over 50 yards.

COMBAT INFANTRYMAN BADGE – Badge awarded by U.S. Army for being personally present and under hostile fire while serving in assigned, primary infantry, or special forces duty in a unit actively engaging the enemy in ground combat.

C-RATIONS – Daily food portions provided by the Army that never spoiled. They consisted of various combinations of canned meat, fruit, and cookies and were often eaten cold under battlefield conditions.

CS GAS GRENADE – A hand grenade that releases tear gas.

DINKS – See Gooks.

DOO-DOO – Excrement, crap, dung, feces or poop.

ELEPHANT GRASS – Six to ten-foot tall, sharp-edged grass found in the highlands of Vietnam. Painful to chop through and easy to get lost in.

FIRE – Gunfire, unless referring specifically to flames.

FO – Forward artillery observer. Soldier who directed artillery or air strikes by radio. He often accompanied the infantry in the field.

FRAG, FRAGGED, FRAGGING – An attempt to kill something or someone, usually with a hand grenade or a Claymore.

FREE-FIRE AREA – An unsettled area with no civilians, where only enemy combat troops and our own were expected to be encountered.

FRIENDLY FIRE – American weapons mistakenly fired into American positions.

G.I. – "Government Issue." The Army labeled everything from boots, to guns, to tanks as government issue. The soldiers adopted this term to refer to themselves.

GOOKS – Slang name for the Viet Cong or North Vietnamese Army, and sometimes for the Vietnamese people in general.

GRUNTS – Infantry soldiers.

GUNG HO – GI slang for zealous, eager and enthusiastic individuals.

HEDGEROWS – Bushes growing tightly together along the edge of a field or rice paddy.

HOOCH – Small structure that the Vietnamese people lived in, made of sticks and straw with a dirt floor.

HOT LZ – A landing zone taking heavy enemy fire when troops came in to land.

HUEY – See Chopper.

HUMP – Slang for marching cross-country with a rucksack or pack.

IN-COUNTRY – On the ground in South Vietnam.

INTEL – Intelligence information as to the supposed current status of affairs.

K.I.A. – Killed in action.

KIT CARSON SCOUT – A former VC or NVA soldier who voluntarily accompanied American units in the field, acting as advisors and interpreters.

KLICK – One kilometer, 1,000 meters, or 1,094 yards.

KP DUTY – Kitchen police or kitchen patrol; assigned work under the kitchen staff.

LZ – Landing zone. Sometimes a firebase with a name (i.e. LZ Bronco), but basically anywhere a helicopter could land.

M16 – Most grunts carried this semi-automatic/full-automatic rifle.

M60 – The 7.62mm squad machine gun of the infantry. Belt-fed, air-cooled, and fired 550 rounds per minute.

M72 LAW – Light anti-tank weapon. A lightweight and accurate 66mm rocket in a disposable fiberglass launcher.

M79 – 40mm grenade launcher. Each grenade weighed about a half-pound, so most grunts didn't want to carry it. Those who did often would swap it for the M16 of a new replacement soldier.

NVA – North Vietnamese Army. The enemy; well-trained and well-disciplined.

P38 – Small can opener that came with C-rations, usually kept on a dog-tag chain or in a pocket.

PUNJI PIT – A hole in the ground about three feet in diameter and 18 feet deep with sharpened "punji" stakes sticking up from the bottom. The stakes were often covered with excrement to cause infections in the wounds of those who fell on them.

PURPLE HEART – Decoration awarded for being wounded or killed in any action against an enemy of the United States or as a result of any act of any such enemy or opposing armed forces.

QUAD-50 – Four .50 caliber machine guns mounted on a platform.

RPG – Rocket-propelled grenade launcher. Soviet or Chinese made, these were armor-penetrating and deadly.

RTO – Radio telephone operator. The soldier who carried a 25-pound radio that kept platoons in touch with the captain, other platoons, and firebases.

RUCKSACK or PACK – A backpack weighing up to 80 pounds, where a soldier carried most of his equipment.

SHAMMING – A soldier making some kind of condition seem worse than it was so he would have an excuse to get out of the field for a while and take it easy.

SHORT-TIMER – Having only a short time left to serve in-country.

SPIDER HOLE – A hole in the ground about two feet in diameter with a camouflaged lid, often connected to tunnels. The enemy could hide, shoot, and be gone from sight before anyone knew what had hit them.

STAND DOWN – A period of time when soldiers were brought to a safe area. Someone else pulled guard and grunts could eat, drink, and sleep all they wanted.

STEM END OF BLADDER – Penis.

TEE-TEE (TI-TI) – Tiny bit, little bit, small, or small amount. Sometimes used to describe how much time left in-country. (See Short-timer.)

TRACK – See APC.

VC – Viet Cong or Vietnamese Communists. The enemy often disguised as civilians. Cruel thugs who harmed anyone that didn't go along with their agenda.

ACKNOWLEDGEMENTS

Heritage is important. In writing this book I want my children, their families, and future generations to know my story. I want to give special recognition to my father Warren, now deceased, who lived the truth; my wife Beth, who believes in me, and always builds me up with her kindness, knowledge, and unending love; my daughter Lisa, who taught me about trust and shows me what graciousness means; my son Bobby, who taught me how to enjoy life again, and gives me good perspective and reasons to laugh and play; my son-in-law Chris, who takes joy in prodding me along and helps me not to take myself too seriously; my daughter-in-law Nicole, whose depth of character brings richness to our family; and my grandchildren Ashley, Caden, Bob G. III, and Wyatt, who fill my life with love and joy, and are an ever-present reminder of my hope for the future.

I would like to give thanks to:

The families of those who have served our country, who don't get near the credit they deserve.

Denver Mills and his staff at the Concord Vet Center; Dr. Joan Kotun at the VA Hospital in Martinez, California; and Gary Villalba and his staff at the Contra Costa County Veterans Department. These wonderful people do more than their jobs call for; they care, restore trust, and help heal.

Pastor Jon McNeff at NorthCreek Church in Walnut Creek, California.

The focus group: Charlie, Christine, Dan, Darryll, Dick, Gil, Greg, Herb, Jeanene, Jerry, Juli, Linda, Marian, Mark, Marla, Mike, Ron, Sara, Virginia, Vonda, and those others who gave their time to review the manuscript and offer us valuable input.

A big thank you to Ken Roberts of F23 whose boundless generosity, energy, and mastery contributed more than I can say; to Robert Pease whose expertise helped me focus my vision; and to Patty Floyd who was wholeheartedly essential in pulling this all together.

A special thanks to my daughter Lisa and wife Beth who have worked endlessly fine-tuning my writing. This book was completed because of their love and dedication. I treasure their help and unwavering devotion.

This will be written for a generation to come,
That a people yet to be created may praise the LORD.
Psalm 102:18

ABOUT THE AUTHOR

Bob Whitworth was born in 1946 in Delano, a small farming community in Central California. He grew up hunting, fishing, and building go-carts. As a teenager, he worked for his dad in the gasoline station their family operated.

Bob was drafted into the U.S. Army on June 14, 1967 at the age of 20. He served with the Americal Division, 21st Infantry, 4th Battalion, 11th Light Infantry Brigade, Delta Company, 2nd Platoon in the Republic of Vietnam from April 1968 to April 1969, and is a recipient of the Bronze Star with "V," the Purple Heart, and the Combat Infantry Badge, as well as other awards. He came home in April of 1969 and married Beth, his sweetheart of two years, one month later.

When Bob came back from the war it was a struggle, as it is for many veterans, to find work that suited him. He held various jobs for the first couple of years but eventually apprenticed with the Steamfitters Local 342 where he worked his way to a General Foreman's position. His 30 years running jobs in heavy construction gave him opportunities to solve problems and work with many different kinds of people from all over the United States.

Bob earned his private pilot's license in 1984. Over the years he has owned three airplanes: a Cessna 150, a Cessna 170 and in 1990 he restored a 1954 Cessna 180. He and Beth have adventured together, flying around the western United States.

After his service in Vietnam, Bob continually struggled with nightmares, haunting memories of the war, and the continuing effects of malaria. He depended on the Bible for answers to his deep questions. He and Beth together sought out whatever help they could find from friends and other resources. Finally, after 30 years, and much persuasion from Beth, Bob again went to the Concord Veterans Center where he found someone running the program who truly cared about Vietnam Vets. Since that time Bob has been an active participant in their efforts to care for veterans.

After retiring as a result of health issues, Bob received a call from one of his Vietnam buddies looking for information about one of the men killed during a battle in which Bob had fought. That battle, as well as his other experiences, were not something Bob normally discussed. But, because his buddy asked him to, he wrote out the story of that time near Tam Ky. Several people read it and encouraged Bob to write more about his service in Vietnam. That's how the story of his tour came to be told.

Although the nightmares, ear ringing, and haunting memories remain, the character Bob has gained from perseverance through the toughest of times has paid rewarding dividends and gives him hope for the future.

Today Bob is a mentor for returning soldiers at his local veterans center. He enjoys hunting, fishing, and traveling with Beth. Bob loves dogs of all kinds, and his German Shorthair, Dallas, can be seen with him almost everywhere he goes.

Bob and Beth live in Concord, California, have two children and four grandchildren.

While in infantry training in Hawaii in 1967, Bob bought a movie camera
and made a leather pouch for it that fastened to his pistol belt.
During his tour in Vietnam, he carried this camera and periodically
was able to get some interesting footage.
Video clips from those movies can be seen on our website.

www.ThroughMyEyesTheBook.com